3-15-60

GOURMET KITCHEN

Evelyn Patterson's
GOURMET
KITCHEN

ABELARD-SCHUMAN

LONDON & NEW YORK

Library of Congress Catalog Card Number: 58-7015

Printed in Great Britain by
Hazell Watson & Viney Ltd., Aylesbury and Slough
for Abelard-Schuman Ltd., 38 Russell Square, London, WC1
and 404 Fourth Avenue, New York 16, N.Y.

Contents

INTRODUCTION
page 9

MEAT & FOWL

FISH

FISH *continued*

OMELETS

VEGETABLES

VEGETABLES *continued*

DESSERT PASTRY

DESSERTS

DESSERTS *continued*

YEAST DOUGHS

QUICK BREADS

Introduction

EVEN men agree that running a house properly is a complicated and demanding task! Some of the duties are routine, many are pure drudgery. But it has always seemed to me a great misfortune that women often regard the preparation of food for a family as falling into both categories. This is especially to be regretted since meal-time is often the only occasion during the day when the family is together.

The task this little book sets itself therefore is to help make family meals and company meals something the lady of the house can take pride in as an outlet for her creative talents. It is certain that if the cook has fun preparing food, those who eat it will also enjoy themselves.

Like my first book, *Meals for Guests*, this is not designed to compete with the many fine basic and special cook-books available today. Nor is this an encyclopedia of gourmet cooking. *Gourmet Kitchen* aims rather at helping the modern wife, the new or the experienced homemaker to develop some basic techniques and to add to her repertoire a select collection of exciting recipes.

A basic assumption of this book is that there is no such thing as *the* gourmet's kitchen. Fine cooking is a very individual matter, and once the fundamental techniques and a reasonable range of recipes are mastered, each cook can't help but create an endless series of exciting variations. Not only the food but also the table setting in any home should reflect the special imagination, taste and whims of that particular house.

The selection of foods presented here has been greatly influenced by my experience in conducting an experimental course in gourmet cooking at the Princeton, New Jersey, Adult School. In large part this book was influenced by the questions repeatedly asked by students who seriously aspired to become fine cooks; questions about cooking techniques as well as requests for specific recipes.

There is often no *one* technique for performing a certain task nor one recipe for a given delicacy. The ones given here are those which in my experience best satisfy the particular wants of many Americans and are most easily managed with the facilities of American food stores and kitchens. Some of the classic recipes for well known exotic dishes are simply too complex for any but a professional chef. Fortunately, considerable experimentation has shown that an elegant substitute can often be made with ingredients and procedures familiar to American women. A general rule that should never be broken is that the ingredients used must be of excellent quality. But not all the ingredients need be expensive. You will be pleased to find how often an expensive item can be combined with low cost ones so that the former highlights the taste and appearance of the finished product.

To add an exciting flair to your efforts, I do recommend a wider variety of herbs, wines and liqueurs than commonly graces the shelves of American kitchens. The initial cost of arranging such a stock may seem a little high, but coupled with a careful method of preparing food, small amounts of these commodities go a long way and—much more important— often permit a considerable saving in the cost of meat. The following seasonings, ever present on the cupboard shelf, will offer a bounty of interesting flavors for your adventures in cooking: thyme, marjoram, basil, tarragon, bay leaf, oregano, dry mustard, peppercorns, cloves, nutmeg, mace, ginger and allspice; also dry white wine, dry red wine, sherry, port, madeira, cointreau, kirsch and brandy.

Undoubtedly there can be found the good cook who can prepare a good meal with very few utensils, but a well equipped kitchen, by reducing the amount of work, adds considerably to the pleasure of preparing food. The most important appliance is of course a properly regulated stove and oven. It is absolutely essential that you be able to know the exact temperature in your oven, that the heat be steady and even, with fine adjustments possible in both the heat of the oven and the burner tops. The other essential items I would list are:

Measuring cups

Measuring spoons

Rotary egg beater

Wire whisk for beating and blending

Wooden spoons for mixing

Rubber scraper

Sharp knives of assorted sizes for cutting and chopping

Meat grinder or food chopper with coarse, medium and fine blades

Moully grater with assorted blades

Mixing bowls of assorted sizes (stainless steel bowls are ideal)

Sauce pans of assorted sizes with tight covers

Skillets of assorted sizes with tight covers (at least one heavy skillet)

Pie pans

Cake pans

Bread tins

Muffin tins and custard cups

Flan rings

Soufflé dishes

Ring molds

Flour sifter

Colander and fine strainer

Pastry blender

Pastry cloth and rolling pin with cover

Wooden block for chopping and cutting

Most of these items seem obvious, but a few may seem superfluous, for example, flan rings and soufflé dishes. To be sure, flans and soufflés can be made without special dishes, but not as successfully. With these items relatively inexpensive, it will be worthwhile to protect your investment in time and energy by using the proper utensils.

Tarts are better when made in flan rings rather than in pie or cake pans, for it is very difficult to remove a tart from such pans. To serve the tart directly from the pan is inconvenient as well as unattractive, but with a flan ring, snap off the ring and the tart is ready to serve, better tasting and delightfully crisp from having been allowed to cool without the ring.

It is also, of course, possible to make a soufflé without a special soufflé dish; it can be baked in an ordinary casserole, but you may be a little disappointed in its texture and appearance. Soufflés should be baked in a ceramic dish with absolutely straight sides. This facilitates the rising. Wiser, too, is the cook who is certain the dish is just the right size for the amount of soufflé—one that will be level-full so that all the rising is done above the rim. The soufflé then exits proudly from the oven towering at least four inches above the dish.

Not essential but very desirable for those who have the space and means are:

Electric mixer (deemed by many as most essential)	Electric blender
	Electric deep fat fryer
Second oven	Marble slab for pastry

As in *Meals for Guests*, these recipes have been planned to serve six portions. I have personally prepared and served each with the most desirable reward a good cook can receive—individual compliments from those served. I hope you enjoy the same happy experience.

EVELYN R. PATTERSON

128 *FitzRandolph Road,*
Princeton, New Jersey

Meat and Fowl

THIS is a carefully selected group of entrée recipes. No attempt has been made to include all categories of meat and fowl. When faced with too many recipes for each type and cut of meat, many of us frequently conclude that picking one is just too difficult, with the result that we often fall back on the method we've always used. So here only those recipes have been chosen which you are not likely to have tried before, which are within your skill, which will not overtax your pocketbook, and, above all, which will surely delight you and those who share your table.

STUFFED BREAST OF VEAL

3 to 4 pounds breast of veal
½ pound chicken liver
¼ pound pork sausage
½ cup dry bread crumbs
½ cup chopped onion (sautéed until tender)
1 clove garlic, crushed
1 tablespoon chopped parsley
1 tablespoon chopped chives or any fresh herb you have
½ cup sliced mushrooms, sautéed in butter until tender
1 beaten egg
Salt and pepper to taste
1 cup dry white wine

Bone the veal. Sauté the chicken liver in butter until tender, about 4 minutes. Remove from pan and chop coarsely.

Mix the chopped liver with the sausage, sautéed onion, garlic, herbs, sautéed mushrooms, salt and pepper, and beaten egg.

Spread this mixture evenly on the veal, leaving a margin of 1 inch around the edge. You may cover with finger sized slices of tongue or ham if you wish to be very elegant. Roll as you would a jelly roll and tie securely with string.

Place in a shallow pan and bake at 375° F. until brown, about 20 minutes. Pour over 1 cup of dry white wine, cover the pan closely and bake for half-hour at 350° F.

Remove the meat from the oven and slice in 1 inch slices, arranging the slices in a slightly overlapping fashion in the serving platter. Strain the pan juices over the meat.

If you wish you may thicken the juice slightly with a little cornstarch dissolved in cold water. Do this on a low flame and add the cornstarch gradually in order not to thicken the juice too much.

Surround the sliced veal roll with mounds of freshly cooked vegetables, preferably of a variety of colors. I suggest carrots, peas, green beans and broiled tomato slices.

BEEF À LA MODE

Boeuf à la mode may be country fare in France, but it is a delicious enough dish for any city. Make a large quantity, serving it hot the first day and cold the next day, when the pan juices will have jelled into a delicious aspic.

4 pounds pot roast of beef	⅛ teaspoon thyme
Salt pork for larding	Pinch of nutmeg
2 tablespoons butter	Piece of cracked veal knuckle
1 cup hot water	about the size of your fist
2 cups dry white wine	¼ cup brandy
Salt and pepper	4 carrots cut into 1 inch pieces
1 large bay leaf	10 small whole onions
Sprig of parsley	3 cloves stuck into one of the onions

Trim fat from the beef. Run 4 or 5 narrow strips of salt pork through the beef with a larding needle. Brown the meat in hot butter in a heavy iron casserole or Dutch oven.

Add the water, wine, herbs, seasoning, and veal knuckle, cover and simmer over a low flame for 2 hours. Add the brandy, carrots, onions and cloves. Simmer for another hour or until very tender. Remove the veal knuckle and cloves. If there is too much sauce, pour it off into another pan, reducing it a little over a high flame.

Slice enough of the beef for one meal, arranging it in a slightly overlapping fashion on a hot serving platter. Arrange the carrots and onions around the slices and strain some of the sauce over the meat.

VEAL IN PORT AND CREAM

Thin slices of tender veal in a deliciously rich sauce.

12 thin slices of veal (2 to 2½ pounds)	1 cup port wine
Salt and pepper	½ tablespoon cornstarch
¼ cup butter	Cold water
2 cups sliced mushrooms	1½ cups light cream

Have the butcher cut veal cutlet or tenderloin in thin slices 4 by 5 inches square and ¼ inch thick. Allow two slices per serving. This cut of veal is called a scallop or escalop. If your butcher is familiar with the term, you can ask for 12 veal scallops.

Salt and pepper the veal slices and brown them on both sides, in a large, heavy skillet in which you have melted the butter. Add more butter if necessary to keep the veal from sticking to the pan. Now add the sliced mushrooms, cover tightly and allow to simmer for 4 minutes. Remove the veal and mushrooms to a serving platter and set aside in a warm place while making the sauce.

Stir the port into the pan and simmer for 3 minutes. Slowly blend in the cornstarch dissolved in a little cold water. Stirring constantly, cook slowly until smooth and thickened. Gently stir in the cream and heat just to the boiling point. The sauce will be medium thick and reddish-brown in colour. Pour the sauce over the veal and mushrooms and serve immediately.

VEAL CHOPS LORRAINE

Veal chops reach their zenith served in this aromatic tasty sauce. Here is truly an unusual blend of the heartiness of German cookery with the delicacy of the French style.

½ cup diced bacon	2 teaspoons butter
6 veal chops—½ inch thick	1 cup stock or bouillon
Salt and pepper	1 cup dry white wine
1 medium onion, finely chopped	2 beaten egg yolks
¼ cup chopped parsley	2 teaspoons lemon juice
2 teaspoons flour	1 teaspoon grated lemon rind

Fry the bacon until crisp in a heavy skillet. Add the seasoned chops and cook for 10 minutes on each side. Remove the chops and bacon to a serving platter and set aside to keep warm while making the sauce.

Pour off the bacon grease leaving just enough to cover the bottom of the skillet. Add the chopped onion and parsley and cook, stirring occasionally, until the onion is soft but not brown. Mix the flour and butter together into a smooth paste and blend them into the juices in the pan. Slowly blend in the stock and wine, stirring constantly. If you have no stock on hand, either veal or beef, dissolve a bouillon cube in a cup of hot water. Simmer for 5 minutes. Now slowly stir a little of the hot sauce into the beaten egg yolks and then gradually stir the warmed yolks into the sauce. Heat through but do not allow the sauce to boil. Reheat the chops and bacon in the sauce for a few minutes if they have become cold. Just before serving stir in the lemon juice and rind. Arrange the chops on a serving platter and cover with the sauce.

VEAL ROLLS IN SOUR CREAM

Veal and sour cream always go well together, but in this are just the right added attractions to make the mixture superb.

18 wafer thin veal slices	½ teaspoon salt
(1½ pounds)	½ teaspoon paprika
2 tablespoons chopped onion	½ teaspoon thyme
2 tablespoons chopped celery	Flour for dredging
3 tablespoons butter	2 cups sour cream
1½ cups soft bread crumbs	3 tablespoons currant jelly
2 tablespoons minced parsley	

Have the butcher cut the veal in very thin slices about 3 inches square. Allow 3 pieces of veal per serving.

Make a filling for the rolls by sautéing the finely chopped onion and celery in the butter until the onion is soft. Add the soft bread crumbs, parsley, salt, paprika and thyme and mix well together.

Spread each of the veal slices with some of the filling. Roll up the squares of veal, fasten with toothpicks and dredge with flour. Sauté the rolls in butter in a heavy skillet until brown on all sides. Gradually add the sour cream to the skillet, cover tightly and cook over low heat for 20 minutes. Taste for seasoning, adding salt and pepper if necessary. Just before serving, stir the currant jelly into the sauce. The whole dish may be made ahead of time without the currant jelly which *must* be added at the last minute.

VEAL IN CHERRY-RAISIN SAUCE

This combination may sound weird, but it is wonderful, and certainly a new taste sensation for your family or guests.

2 pounds veal cutlet, ½ inch	Flour for dredging
thick	⅓ cup butter
Salt and pepper	2 cups heavy cream

1 cup pitted canned black or red sweet cherries	½ cup seedless raisins Boiled rice

Cut the veal into serving pieces, salt and pepper each piece and dredge with flour. Melt the butter in a heavy skillet, brown the veal on both sides, pour on the cream, add the cherries and raisins, cover the skillet closely and simmer for ½ hour or until the veal is tender. If the sauce is too thin, mix a bit of cornstarch in cold water and gradually add it to the sauce until you have the desired consistency. Serve with fluffy boiled rice.

VEAL CUTLET WITH HAM AND SWISS CHEESE

This is the simple but delicious Wiener Schnitzel glorified and made more delicious by the mere laying on of ham and cheese.

6 slices veal cutlet, ¼ inch thick (2 pounds) Salt and pepper 2 beaten eggs 2 tablespoons water	Fine dry bread crumbs ¼ cup butter 6 slices prosciutto ham or thinly sliced baked ham 6 slices Swiss cheese

Cut the cutlets into approximately 4 by 5 inch pieces. Season with salt and pepper. Beat the eggs with the water. Dip each veal slice into the beaten eggs and then in the fine bread crumbs, covering them evenly with the crumbs. Chill in refrigerator for at least 30 minutes. Sauté the slices in butter until golden brown on both sides. Arrange the breaded veal in a shallow baking dish, place a thin slice of ham over each slice and then a slice of cheese on top of the ham. Put into a 350° oven until the cheese is just melted. Serve immediately.

VEAL MARENGO

An easy way to turn an inexpensive cut of veal into an elegant dish.

4 large ripe tomatoes
1½ pounds cubed veal (1 inch cubes)
3 tablespoons cooking oil
1 large onion, coarsely chopped
2 tablespoons flour

1 cup dry white wine
2 cups chicken stock
1 clove garlic, finely chopped
Salt and pepper to taste
1 cup thickly sliced mushrooms
1 tablespoon butter

Plunge the tomatoes into rapidly boiling water and keep boiling until the skins begin to break (about 1 minute). Remove tomatoes, cool quickly under cold water, peel off the skins and remove the hard core. Cut into chunks. If tomatoes are out of season, use the canned ones.

Heat the oil in a heavy pan, add the cubed veal and brown on all sides. Add the chopped onion and tomatoes. Cook for 2 minutes and then stir in the flour until evenly blended. Stirring gently, gradually add the white wine and the chicken stock. If you have no chicken stock on hand, use either canned stock or 2 chicken bouillon cubes dissolved in a cup of hot water. Add the finely chopped garlic. Taste for seasoning. Cover the pan tightly and allow to simmer over low heat for 1 hour or until the meat is tender. In a separate pan sauté the mushrooms in butter until tender, about 5 minutes. Add them to the meat just before serving. This dish is best, I think, served with fluffy boiled rice.

GROUND VEAL AND PORK CAKES

These cakes are most unusual both in texture and flavor and smothered in a smooth rich sauce they make a delicious dish.

1 pound ground lean veal	⅛ teaspoon nutmeg
1 pound ground lean pork	½ teaspoon salt
4 large peeled potatoes	½ teaspoon pepper
1 large onion	3 tablespoons butter
1¼ cups cream	1 cup rich chicken stock
2 tablespoons finely chopped	2 tablespoons flour
parsley	1 teaspoon lemon juice

Run the ground veal, pork, potatoes and onion through a food chopper twice, using the fine blade. If you take your peeled potatoes and onion to the meat market with you the butcher will do this part of the job for you. Mix these ingredients well with ½ cup of the cream, parsley, nutmeg, salt and pepper. Shape the mixture into cakes 1 inch thick and 2 inches across. Sauté the cakes in butter until brown on both sides. Add ¼ cup of the cream and the chicken stock to the pan, cover tightly and simmer for 30 minutes. Remove the cakes to a serving dish. Mix the flour with ½ cup cream and then stir it slowly into the juices in the pan. Stir and cook over low heat until the sauce is smooth and thickened. Stir in the lemon juice and pour the sauce over the cakes.

SWEETBREADS

Sweetbreads, as I said in *Meals for Guests*, are a delicacy much neglected by the American housewife and cook. This is regrettable for they are not difficult to prepare and are not costly. Although the price per pound may seem high, a pound goes a long way for there is very little waste. They can be prepared in many ways but the first steps, parboiling and chilling, are always the same. The directions for this procedure will be given here and not repeated in each subsequent recipe.

Plunge the sweetbreads into cold water and let them stand for 45 minutes. Drain and put them into boiling water seasoned with 1 teaspoon salt, 2 tablespoons lemon juice, 2 slices onion,

1 stalk celery and a bay leaf. Simmer slowly for 20 minutes. Drain and again plunge them into cold water. Let them stand until well chilled. Remove the membrane and the fine covering tissue. The sweetbreads are now ready to be used. They may be stored in the refrigerator for several hours but they should not be kept for more than one day.

SAUTÉED SWEETBREADS À LA CRÈME

Sweetbreads in a "heady" sauce flavored to bring out the subtle delicacy of the sweetbreads. Exciting but never overpowering.

2 pair sweetbreads	1 pound mushrooms, sliced
Flour for dredging	¼ cup sherry
4 tablespoons butter	1 tablespoon lemon juice
2 tablespoons warm brandy	1 cup heavy cream
Salt and pepper	3 cups croûtons
⅛ teaspoon nutmeg	Butter

Parboil and chill the sweetbreads according to directions on page 20. Slice the sweetbreads and dredge lightly with flour. Sauté the slices in butter until golden brown. Pour the warmed brandy over them and set aflame. When the flame has burned out, season the sweetbreads with salt, pepper and nutmeg. Add the sliced mushrooms, cover and simmer for 4 minutes. Stir in the sherry and simmer for another 4 minutes. Gradually add the lemon juice and cream. Heat through but do not allow it to boil. Place the sweetbreads in the center of a platter, cover them with the sauce and surround by the browned croûtons.

The croûtons may be made well in advance and heated in the oven just before serving. To make the croûtons, cut fresh or semi-fresh bread into small cubes, ¼ inch square. Have the bottom of a heavy skillet covered with bubbling butter, add the cubes of bread and toss lightly with a fork. Shake the skillet over medium heat and turn the cubes occasionally until they are golden brown on all sides.

SWEETBREADS IN PORT AND CREAM

Sweetbreads in a pretty pinkish sauce of hauntingly fragile flavor to complement the delicateness of sweetbreads.

2 pairs sweetbreads	Salt to taste
4 tablespoons butter	1 pound mushrooms, sliced
1 cup port wine	4 tablespoons butter
1½ cups heavy cream	2 teaspoons cornstarch
½ cup strong chicken stock	Cold water

Parboil and chill sweetbreads according to directions on page 20. Divide the sweetbreads into bite size pieces. Melt the butter in a heavy skillet, add the sweetbreads and sauté until golden brown. Add the port, cover the skillet tightly and simmer for 5 minutes. Remove from heat and gradually stir in the heavy cream and chicken stock. If you have no stock, use canned chicken consommé or dissolve 1 chicken bouillon cube in ½ cup hot water. Taste for seasoning, adding salt if necessary. Sauté the sliced mushrooms in butter, covered, for 5 minutes. Add to sweetbreads. Cover the skillet and simmer over low heat for 15 minutes. Continue cooking slowly as you gradually add the cornstarch which has been mixed with a little cold water, stopping when you have the thickness desired. The sauce must hold together but not be thick and gummy. This dish is especially good served with wild rice, but it also goes well with toast triangles.

BRAISED SWEETBREADS

This dish has a tasty aromatic sauce which points up the flavor of the sweetbreads.

2 pair sweetbreads
Salt and pepper
2 tablespoons butter
1 medium onion, sliced
1 carrot, sliced
1 bay leaf

½ teaspoon thyme
4 sprigs parsley
½ cup sherry
1 cup chicken stock or bouillon
½ pound mushrooms, sliced
2 tablespoons butter

Parboil, chill and trim sweetbreads according to directions on page 20. Season with salt and pepper. Put the butter in an ovenproof skillet or casserole, add the sliced onion, carrot, bay leaf, thyme and parsley. Place the sweetbreads on top of the vegetables and cook over low heat until the vegetables begin to turn golden. Add the sherry and chicken stock or bouillon. Put the dish, uncovered, into a 375° oven and bake for 45 minutes, basting well every 15 minutes. At the end of this time the sweetbreads should be well browned and glazed. The sauce should be slightly thickened. If it is not, stir in about 1 teaspoon cornstarch dissolved in a little sherry and simmer for a few minutes. Arrange the sweetbreads on a serving platter, strain the sauce over them and garnish with the sliced mushrooms that you have sautéed in butter until tender.

CHICKEN LIVERS NORDAISE

If you rarely serve chicken livers, see how easy they are to prepare—and how glamorous. Here is a sample to make you take notice.

1 pound chicken livers
4 tablespoons butter
2 tablespoons flour
1 cup canned chicken consommé
   or bouillon
½ cup sherry wine

Salt and pepper
2 cups sliced mushroom
2 tablespoons butter
2 tablespoons chopped parsley
Boiled rice or toast

Heat the butter in a skillet. Add the chicken livers and sautè quickly until well browned. Remove the livers from pan.

Gradually add the flour to the drippings in the pan and then slowly blend in the consommé and sherry. Simmer, continuing to stir, until the sauce thickens. Season to taste with salt and pepper. Sauté the mushrooms in butter in a separate pan. Add sautéed mushrooms and parsley to the chicken livers and simmer until they are thoroughly heated. Serve on rice or on toast.

CHICKEN LIVERS IN SOUR CREAM

2 tablespoons butter	1 cup sour cream
1 onion, chopped fine	¼ cup strong chicken stock or
1 tablespoon parsley, chopped	bouillon
¼ tablespoon sweet marjoram	Salt and pepper
1½ pounds chicken livers	Boiled rice

Melt the butter in a skillet, add the onion and sauté until golden. Add the parsley, marjoram and chicken livers. Brown the livers quickly over high heat, then lower the heat and gradually stir in the sour cream. Simmer gently for 5 minutes. Add the strong chicken stock or bouillon and continue to simmer for 3 more minutes. Taste for seasoning and if necessary, add salt and pepper. Serve piping hot with fluffy boiled rice. Garnish with sprigs of parsley.

KIDNEYS FLAMBÉ

The lowly kidney when treated properly can hold its own with the most expensive of meat as gourmet fare.

6 veal kidneys	Salt and pepper
3 tablespoons butter	¼ teaspoon dry mustard
½ pound sliced mushrooms	⅔ cup heavy cream
3 tablespoons brandy, warmed	6 slices toast

Clean and skin the kidneys and cut into bite size pieces. Sauté the kidneys in butter over a high flame. Push the kidneys to the side of the pan, lower the heat, and sauté the sliced mushrooms for 4 minutes or until tender. Pour on the warmed brandy and set aflame. When the flame dies out, season to taste with salt and pepper and add the mustard. Mix well. Arrange the kidneys and mushrooms on the slices of toast. Stir the heavy cream into the pan juices and heat thoroughly, being careful not to boil. Pour the sauce over the kidneys and mushrooms and serve.

CHICKEN IN WINE SAUCE

Chicken smothered in this fragrant wine sauce will please even the most exacting of epicures.

3 to 4 pounds roasting chicken cut into serving pieces	Bouquet garni—bay leaf, thyme, parsley and basil
Salt and pepper	1 tablespoon butter
1 onion, minced	2 tablespoons flour
4 tablespoons butter	⅔ cup heavy cream
1 cup dry white wine	2 tablespoons sherry
1 cup chicken stock or bouillon	1 teaspoon brandy
½ cup mushroom liquor	1 cup cooked or canned sliced
1 clove garlic, chopped	mushrooms

Remove skin from the chicken. Season the pieces of chicken with salt and pepper and sauté them with the minced onion in butter over a low flame until light golden brown. Add the wine, chicken stock and mushroom liquor. If you are using fresh mushrooms, which are better, you may obtain the liquor by boiling them for 3 minutes in a small amount of water and a few drops of lemon juice. Add the garlic and a bouquet garni (bay leaf, thyme, basil and parsley tied up in a small piece of cheesecloth). Cover the skillet closely and cook over a low flame until chicken is tender, about 1 hour.

Remove the cooked chicken to a platter and keep warm.

Remove the bouquet garni and blend into the sauce a paste made of the butter and flour. Simmer until sauce is slightly thickened. Gradually stir in the heavy cream, sherry and brandy. Cover the chicken on the platter with the mushrooms and pour the sauce over all. Accompany the chicken with fluffy boiled rice, boiled noodles or baked potatoes.

CHICKEN BREASTS IN CREAM
AND BRANDY

A beautiful pink sauce over tender breast of chicken makes a dish to delight the eye as well as the palate.

6 small chicken breasts split (about 4 pounds)	3 tablespoons brandy, warmed
Salt and pepper	1 tablespoon flour
½ cup butter	1½ cups heavy cream, heated
½ pound mushrooms, sliced	1¼ teaspoons tomato paste

Season the chicken breasts with salt and pepper and cook them in butter in a heavy skillet over moderate heat for about 30 minutes. When the chicken is brown and tender, add the sliced mushrooms and cook for another 5 minutes. Pour on the warmed brandy and touch with a lighted match to blaze it. When the flame dies out, remove the chicken and mushrooms to a platter and set aside to keep warm. Blend the flour into the juices in the pan. Slowly stir in the hot heavy cream mixed with the tomato paste. Simmer the sauce gently for 10 minutes. Taste for seasoning. Pour the lovely pinkish sauce through a strainer over the chicken and mushrooms. Serve immediately.

CHICKEN CITRON

A most elegant way to serve chicken and most simple to prepare. The combination of flavors is interesting and delicious.

6 pounds frying chicken or 4 to 5 pounds chicken legs or breasts
½ cup butter
2 tablespoons sherry
2 tablespoons white wine
Grated rind of one medium orange
Grated rind of one large lemon
3 teaspoons lemon juice
Salt and pepper to taste
1½ cups light cream
4 tablespoons grated Parmesan cheese
Boiled rice

Cut up the chicken as for frying; remove the skin. Sauté the chicken in a heavy skillet in the foaming butter until golden brown all over. Cover with a tight lid and continue to cook over low heat until tender, about 20 minutes. Remove the chicken from the pan. Stir the sherry and white wine into the pan drippings. Add the grated lemon and orange rinds, lemon juice and salt and pepper. Stir in the cream slowly. Return the chicken to the skillet and shake over low heat for 5 minutes. Arrange the chicken on a serving platter, cover with sauce and sprinkle with Parmesan cheese. Serve with fluffy boiled rice. The sauce will be thin. I think it is better this way; however, if you prefer a thicker sauce, dissolve a bit of cornstarch in cold water, add it gradually to the sauce and cook gently until you have the consistency you prefer.

BREAST OF CHICKEN GISMONDE

A simple dish, without sauce, whose piquancy belies its simplicity.

6 chicken breasts
Salt and pepper
Flour for dredging
2 eggs
1 tablespoon water
½ cup grated Parmesan cheese
1 cup fine bread crumbs
½ cup butter
2 pounds cooked spinach
1 tablespoon lemon juice
1 pound mushrooms, sliced
2 tablespoons butter
3 tablespoons chopped parsley

Remove the skin and bones from the chicken breasts. Split the breasts in half down the middle and pound each half to flatten it. Season with salt and pepper and dredge each piece with flour. Beat the eggs slightly with a fork; add 1 tablespoon water. Dip the floured chicken into the egg mixture and then roll in a mixture of the Parmesan cheese and bread crumbs. Chill for at least 30 minutes. Sauté the breaded chicken in hot butter until delicately brown on both sides.

While chicken is cooking, purée the hot cooked spinach and season it with the lemon juice. Pile the spinach on a platter and arrange the tender brown chicken on it. Set aside to keep hot. Add more butter to the skillet and sauté the sliced mushrooms until tender. Arrange the mushrooms on top of the chicken breasts. Now melt the additional 2 tablespoons of butter and pour over the platter. Sprinkle with chopped parsley.

ARROZ VALENCIA

This Spanish recipe, combining chicken, seafood and ham, well deserves its popularity. Heartiness and unusual flavor characterize this complete meal in a dish.

½ cup olive oil
1 large onion, chopped
2 green peppers, coarsely chopped
1 chicken, about 3 pounds, skinned, boned and cut into large cubes
½ pound ham cut into strips
5 tomatoes, peeled and quartered, or 1 large can of tomatoes

1 pound cooked fresh shrimp
1 small (8 oz.) can heart of artichokes (may be omitted)
4 cloves garlic
1 cup stock or bouillon
2 bay leaves
Salt and pepper
1½ cups uncooked rice
1 small (6 oz.) can pimientoes

Heat the olive oil, add the onion and green pepper and sauté until tender. Add the chicken that you have skinned, boned and cut into cubes, and the strips of ham. Sauté until the chicken turns golden. Add the cooked shrimp, the tomatoes and artichoke hearts. Pound the garlic fine or put it through a garlic press and add it together with the stock. Add the bay leaves and season with salt and pepper. Cover closely and simmer until the chicken is very tender, about 50 minutes.

While the chicken is cooking, boil the rice until fluffy and tender. Drain and spread on a platter to cool. A few minutes before serving, add the rice to the chicken mixture a little at a time, heating thoroughly. Pile the savory mixture high on a platter and garnish with pimientoes. The chicken mixture and the rice may be prepared in advance and combined and heated just before serving.

GARLIC FRIED CHICKEN

Fried chicken is a tried and true standby. And it is good. To make the good better, try the following variation.

2 small frying chickens cut into serving pieces	½ teaspoon salt
1 cup sour cream	¼ teaspoon pepper
2 tablespoons lemon juice	¼ teaspoon celery salt
¼ teaspoon Worcestershire sauce	⅛ teaspoon paprika
1 large clove garlic, pounded or put through a press	Flour for dredging
	Butter for frying

Wipe the pieces of chicken with a damp cloth and place them in a bowl that has a tight fitting cover. Mix all the other ingredients together and pour them over the chicken, taking care that all the pieces are covered. Cover the bowl tightly and allow it to stand in the refrigerator for at least 12 hours. When ready to fry, lift the pieces out of the sauce and dredge them with flour. Fry until fork tender in a heavy skillet over a low flame in about an inch of butter, turning frequently to prevent burning. If you prefer you can deep fat fry the chicken.

CHICKEN IN PORT AND CREAM

Chicken in this creamy, delicately flavored sauce will whet the dullest appetite. The intricate flavor combination belies the ease of preparation.

2 small frying chickens
Salt and pepper
⅔ cup butter
1½ cups chicken stock or bouillon
1 pound mushrooms, sliced

2 tablespoons flour
2 cups heavy cream
½ cup port wine
4 cups boiled rice or boiled wild rice

Cut chicken into serving pieces and remove the skin. Sauté the chicken in ½ cup butter until golden brown. Pour on the stock and simmer, covered, until the chicken is tender, about 30 minutes. While chicken is cooking, sauté the mushrooms in the remaining butter. Remove chicken from pan, stir in the flour dissolved in a little of the cream. Gradually stir in the cream. Add the mushrooms and the port. Return the chicken to the sauce and simmer for 5 minutes. To serve, arrange the chicken in a mound on a platter and pour the sauce and mushrooms over it. Make a border around the edge of the platter of either wild rice or white rice.

COUNTRY CAPTAIN'S CHICKEN

A hearty chicken dish with enough of an air to be party fare. It is as good to look at as it is to eat.

4 pounds frying chicken
Flour for dredging
Salt and pepper
½ cup butter and vegetable
   shortening
2 onions, chopped fine
2 green peppers, chopped fine

1 clove garlic, chopped fine
1 teaspoon salt
½ teaspoon pepper
2 teaspoons curry powder
4 cups canned tomatoes
½ tablespoon chopped parsley
½ teaspoon powdered thyme

1 cup almonds, blanched and slivered	¼ cup currants
2 tablespoons butter	3 cups boiled rice

Have the chickens cut into serving pieces, remove the skin. Dredge the chicken in flour seasoned with salt and pepper. Fry the chicken in hot butter and shortening until golden brown. Remove it from the pan and set aside. Add to the pan the chopped onion, pepper and garlic and cook slowly until tender. Add the salt, pepper, curry powder, tomatoes, parsley and thyme and simmer for 5 minutes. Put the browned pieces of chicken into a roaster or big casserole, pour the tomato sauce over it. It should be just covered with sauce. If more sauce is needed, add water or stock. Cover the dish tightly and bake at 350° for 1 hour. Sauté almonds in butter until just golden colored.

Arrange the chicken in the center of a platter, surround with a border of fluffy boiled rice. Add the currants to the sauce, cook for 1 minute and pour the sauce over the chicken and rice. Sprinkle with the slivered almonds.

CHICKEN BREASTS À LA BLANCHE

A twist of the wrist and you have a dish. Maybe a simplification when applied to this recipe, but not very much of one. These chicken breasts are easier to prepare than ordinary fried chicken, but no one eating them will believe it, for they are truly in the epicure's class.

6 small chicken breasts	Salt and pepper
Flour for dredging	2 tablespoons currant jelly
½ cup butter	2 tablespoons grated Parmesan cheese
4 tablespoons warm sherry	
1 teaspoon tomato paste	2 cups small whole mushrooms (or sliced mushrooms)
2 tablespoons flour	
1 cup chicken stock	¼ cup butter
1½ cups sour cream	Boiled rice

Bone the chicken breasts. This is a task any obliging butcher will perform for you if you remember to ask him when buying the breasts. Dredge the breasts in flour and brown them in butter or margarine. Pour on the sherry. Mix the tomato paste and flour together and stir them into the pan. Gradually stir in the stock and simmer until the sauce begins to thicken. Slowly stir in the sour cream. Season with salt, pepper, currant jelly and cheese. Cover the pan closely and simmer over low heat for $\frac{1}{2}$ hour. While the chicken is cooking, sauté the mushrooms in butter. Cover the mushrooms while sautéing; they should be tender in about 5 minutes. Arrange the chicken breasts on a platter, cover with the sauce and garnish the whole with the sautéed mushrooms. Serve with boiled rice.

LAMB CASSEROLE

A meal in one dish that is a thing of beauty, combining a most interesting variety of textures and flavors.

3 pounds shoulder lamb, boned and cut into inch cubes	$\frac{1}{2}$ pound small mushrooms
4 tablespoons butter	1 teaspoon tomato paste
2 tablespoons brandy, warmed	$\frac{1}{4}$ cup concentrated stock or Bovril
6 carrots cut into 1 inch pieces	3 tablespoons flour
1 pound small white onions, peeled	1 cup stock
1 pound fresh peas or 1 package frozen peas	$\frac{1}{2}$ cup sherry
$\frac{1}{2}$ pound fresh beans cut french style or 1 package frozen french style beans	Salt and pepper
	2 large tomatoes, peeled and quartered
	2 tablespoons chopped chives

Brown the cubes of lamb in the 2 tablespoons of butter. Pour on the warmed brandy and set aflame. When the flame dies out, remove the meat from the pan and set aside. Add the remaining 2 tablespoons butter to the pan and put in the carrots and onions. Brown these vegetables quickly over high heat.

Lower heat and add the mushrooms, peas and beans. Remove pan from the heat and stir in the tomato paste, concentrated stock and flour. Gradually add the sherry and stock, return to low heat and stir until the mixture comes to a boil. Return lamb to the pan, season, cover closely and cook over low heat for about an hour or until the meat is very tender. Put into a serving dish. Cover the top with the peeled and quartered tomatoes and sprinkle all over with the chopped chives.

LAMB AND EGGPLANT KEBAB

This is a very popular Turkish dish. Lamb and eggplant are great favorites in the Middle East and they go well together. This dish is colorful and tasty, hearty without being heavy.

2 pounds boneless lamb shoulder or leg	1 medium eggplant (1 pound) or 3 of the long (6 inch) narrow variety
Salt and pepper	
2 large onions, sliced	⅓ cup tomato purée
3 tablespoons olive oil or butter	1 cup stock
	3 tomatoes peeled and quartered

Cut lamb into 1½ inch square cubes. Season the lamb cubes with salt and pepper and brown them with the sliced onion in the oil or butter. Cut peeled eggplant into 1½ inch chunks, add to the lamb and allow them to brown slightly. Pour in the tomato purée and stock, cover and simmer gently for 45 minutes. Do not stir unnecessarily as the eggplant will become mashed. Add the quartered tomatoes to the pan only 5 minutes before serving to retain their shape and fresh texture. The Turks serve this dish with a rice pilaf.

GIEUVEITCH

A simple Greek dish of lamb, tomatoes and spaghetti.

3 pounds boneless baby lamb, shoulder or leg	½ cup butter
Lemon juice	6 tomatoes, peeled and sliced
Salt and pepper	2 cups hot water
	½ pound thin spaghetti

Have lamb in one piece or cut into thick slices. Rub the lamb well with lemon juice. Season with salt and pepper. Place the lamb in a shallow (about 2 inch deep) baking dish. An earthenware dish is ideal. Dot the meat with butter and then cover it with the slices of tomato. Bake at 375° F. until brown, about 20 minutes. Then add the hot water and continue baking until almost done, about 25 minutes. Add the spaghetti and bake until the spaghetti is cooked and the lamb is tender, about 20 minutes.

BEEF PATTIES IN WINE

Ground beef when correctly handled can take its place with most any cut of meat without apology.

2 slices stale bread, crumbled	Salt and pepper
⅔ cup milk	Dash of nutmeg
1½ pounds ground beef	3 tablespoons butter
2 onions, finely chopped	3 tablespoons chopped parsley
4 eggs, beaten	⅔ cup dry white wine
2 tablespoons uncooked farina or cream of wheat	

Soak the crumbled stale bread in the milk. Add the other ingredients except the parsley and wine. Mix well. Allow to stand for at least 1 hour. Shape the mixture into cakes about 1 inch thick and 3 inches in diameter. Cook them slowly in butter in a heavy skillet, covered, for about 10 minutes on each side. The cakes should be brown and crusty on the outside and light and airy inside. Add the wine and parsley to the skillet and cook for 3 minutes longer. Arrange the cakes on a platter and pour the wine sauce over them.

PEPPER STEAK

Many cooks contend that it is criminal to tamper with a good steak. They have their point, but this is delicious tampering and gives variety when you do not want "just plain steak".

3 pounds steak at least 1½ inches thick
Salt and coarse ground black pepper
⅛ cup butter
¼ cup olive oil

½ cup dry white wine
½ cup strong stock or bouillon
½ tablespoon cornstarch
Cold water
⅛ cup cognac

Rub the steaks well with coarsely ground black pepper and salt. Heat the butter and olive oil in a large heavy skillet over high heat. Sear the steaks on both sides, turn down the heat and cook until you have the desired doneness, about 7 minutes on each side for rare steak and 15 minutes for well done. Remove the steak to a serving platter and set aside to keep warm. Add the wine and stock to the pan, stirring to combine with the pan juices. Mix the cornstarch with a little cold water, slowly stir into the sauce and cook until you have the thickness desired. The sauce should not be too thick. Add the cognac, stir well and pour over the steaks. Serve immediately.

STEAK BORDELAISE

One thing that is better than a good steak is a good steak served with bordelaise sauce. A good steak can stand on its own merits but occasionally it is interesting and impressive to gild the lily. A bordelaise sauce does just this. It enhances a steak's goodness and even improves it should the meat be a bit inferior.

2 slices bacon, minced
1 tablespoon butter

1 tablespoon minced shallot or onion

2 tablespoons minced ham
1 small clove garlic, minced
1 cup beef stock
1 teaspoon beef extract
Bouquet garni of bay leaf, thyme, marjoram, parsley

½ cup claret
2 tablespoons fine bread crumbs
¼ pound beef marrow, sliced
Salt and pepper
3 pounds beef steak

In this recipe plan to grill or sauté your steak to desired doneness after the sauce has been prepared.

Start frying the bacon in butter, add the shallot or onion, ham and garlic and brown slowly. Add the beef stock and extract, wine and bouquet garni tied in a small piece of cheesecloth and simmer for 30 minutes. Remove the bouquet and add the bread crumbs, salt and pepper. Simmer until sauce thickens. Drop the marrow slices in boiling salted water and immediately remove them with a strainer or slotted spoon. Arrange the marrow slices on top of the steak and pour the sauce over all.

EASY BORDELAISE SAUCE FOR STEAK

This simplified version of bordelaise sauce will be acceptable to all but the most exacting of gourmets. It is so easy to make that you will find yourself making it not only for steaks but also to dress up left-over roast beef or veal.

½ cup red wine
1 small onion, chopped
¼ teaspoon salt
¼ teaspoon pepper
⅛ teaspoon marjoram
⅛ teaspoon thyme

1 bay leaf
½ cup strong consommé or bouillon
¼ teaspoon lemon juice
2 teaspoons chopped parsley
2 teaspoons butter

Combine the wine, chopped onion, salt, pepper, marjoram, thyme and bay leaf and simmer over low heat until the wine is reduced to half, or about ¼ cup. Add the consommé or bouillon and continue to simmer for 10 minutes. It should be a bit thickened and very strongly flavored. If you feel that the sauce is too runny, add a bit of cornstarch mixed with a little cold water and simmer until you get the consistency you desire. Strain the sauce and stir in the lemon juice, parsley and butter. Pour over your sautéed or grilled steak or left-over meat which you have reheated.

STUFFED PASTA À L'ITALIENNE

Eating surveys all show that spaghetti and sauce stand near the top of the favorite food list. The standard spaghetti and sauce is good, but the same ingredients presented in a varied form can be a treat. This stuffed pasta, though a bit more laborious to make, is so attractive and so tasty that you will find it worth the extra effort.

Take the large tubular pasta (rigatoni, tufoli or zitoni), stuff with a well seasoned meat mixture, bake with tomato sauce and cheese and you have a combination to win you plaudits. This can be made well in advance and reheated at time of serving.

1 pound large tubular pasta	1 recipe tomato sauce
Salt	1 pound mozzarella cheese
1 tablespoon cooking oil	1 cup grated Parmesan cheese
1 recipe meat stuffing	

Prepare the sauce and meat stuffing according to recipes given on page 38. Put the pasta into a large kettle of rapidly boiling water to which you have added salt and 1 tablespoon cooking oil. Cook for about ten minutes or until tender but still firm. The oil is added to keep the pasta from sticking together. Drain the pasta and put it into a pan of very cold water. Lift out each piece carefully with a slotted spoon as you are ready to stuff it.

TOMATO SAUCE

2 large onions, chopped
1 large clove garlic, minced or
   pressed
⅛ cup olive oil
3 cups canned tomatoes or 6 large
   fresh tomatoes

1 six ounce can tomato paste
1 cup water
Salt and pepper to taste
1 bay leaf
¼ teaspoon oregano

Brown the onion and garlic in the olive oil. Add the remaining ingredients, stir until well blended, cover and simmer over low heat, stirring from time to time, for 1 hour.

MEAT STUFFING

½ pound ground beef
½ pound ground veal
1 cup mozzarella, cut into cubes
¼ cup grated Parmesan cheese,
   use the remainder to top dish

2 whole eggs
3 tablespoons chopped parsley
½ teaspoon salt
¼ teaspoon pepper

Mix all these ingredients together well, using the fingers. Save remaining mozzarella cheese to use as directed when preparing the casserole.

TO PREPARE THE CASSEROLE

Cover the bottom of a large, 2 quart, casserole with tomato sauce, then add a layer of the stuffed pasta, using one-third of it. Cover the pasta with slivers of mozzarella, cover with sauce and repeat layers until all the pasta, mozzarella cheese and sauce have been used, finishing off with a top layer of sauce sprinkled with the grated Parmesan cheese. Bake at 350° for 1 hour.

BEEF SEMI STROGANOFF

This dish grew our of hunger for stroganoff and a cut of beef not up to real stroganoff requirements. It turned out to be worthy of a name of its own, earning special commendation as the mainstay of a buffet dinner or supper.

2 onions, chopped fine
¼ cup butter
2 pounds round steak cut into fine strips
Salt and pepper to taste
Flour for dredging
1 can condensed tomato soup

1 cup sliced mushrooms sautéed or
1 six ounce can mushrooms
1 tablespoon prepared mustard
2 tablespoons dark brown sugar
Dash Worcestershire sauce
1½ cups sour cream

Brown the onions in butter in a heavy skillet. Salt and pepper the thin strips of beef and dredge them lightly with flour, add to the onions and sauté until well browned. Add the soup, mushrooms, mustard, brown sugar, Worcestershire sauce, sour cream and salt and pepper to taste. Mix well, cover tightly and simmer over low heat for 1 hour. Serve with rice or noodles.

SMOTHERED BEEF STRIPS

An unusual hearty dish that is easy to prepare. You will have many requests to repeat this one.

2 pounds round steak cut into thin, ⅛ inch, strips
Salt and pepper
Flour for dredging
¼ cup butter
2 carrots, diced fine
1 large onion, diced fine
2 stalks celery, diced fine

½ pound mushrooms, chopped fine
2 tablespoons parsley, chopped
1 tablespoon flour
1 cup beef stock
2 cups sour cream
1 tablespoon chopped capers
Boiled wide noodles

Season the thin strips of steak with salt and pepper and dredge with flour. Sauté the steak and all the diced vegetables in hot butter for 5 minutes. Sprinkle with flour and stir until the flour is all absorbed. Add enough beef stock to cover the meat and vegetables, cover the pan and allow to simmer until the meat is tender, about 30 minutes. Spoon off the fat, add the sour cream and capers. Heat thoroughly and serve with boiled wide noodles.

ARMENIAN DOLMAS

Dolmas, stuffed vegetables, are commonly served throughout the Middle and Near Eastern countries. The method of preparation varies slightly from one country to another. I will give the Armenian and Turkish versions, there being the biggest difference between the recipes from these two sources.

2 pounds lean lamb, ground	6 medium tomatoes
1 pound lean beef, ground	6 medium green peppers
1 large onion	3 small eggplants or 6 small
¼ cup cracked wheat	zucchini
¾ cup uncooked rice	½ pound grape leaves (about 50
Salt and pepper	leaves)
1 pound lamb bones	1 cup beef stock or bouillon

Mix the ground lamb and beef. Grate the onion into it and mix in the rice, cracked wheat, salt and pepper. If cracked wheat is unavailable, use 1 cup rice. Next, place the bones on the bottom of a very large casserole or Dutch oven. Count out 6 grape leaves for each serving and roll about 1 tablespoon of the meat mixture in each leaf, fold to look like little cigars with the ends folded over so that the meat is securely contained. Place a tightly fitted layer of these rolled leaves over the lamb bones, using ½ of the prepared leaves for this. Scoop out the centers of the green peppers, tomatoes and eggplant or zuhccini, being careful to keep the skins intact. Reserve the tomato pulp for the sauce. Fill the hollowed vegetables with the meat mixture and arrange them on top of the grapeleaf rolls. Fit them closely together so that they will not tip or break up. Place the remaining filled grape leaves over the filled vegetables and pour over all the stock mixed with the tomato pulp. Cover with plain flat grape leaves and place a plate on top to weight them down. Bake at 350° for 2 hours. Remove the plate and cover of grape leaves. Carefully lift out and arrange the Dolmas on a platter. Serve with hot crusty bread and a tossed green salad.

TURKISH DOLMAS

3 tablespoons olive oil	1½ pounds ground meat, beef or
2 medium onions, chopped fine	lamb
1½ cups uncooked rice	Whole tomatoes, peppers, zucchini
3 cups stock, boiling	and/or eggplant
Salt and pepper	Stock to cover
½ teaspoon sage or dill	Yogurt
2 tablespoons chopped parsley	

You may stuff one or more kinds of vegetables depending on your taste. You may omit the ground meat from the stuffing and use the rice stuffed vegetables as an accompaniment to a roast or to chops.

Heat the oil in a skillet, add the onions and sauté until soft. Add the rice and fry until golden brown. Pour on the boiling stock—it will splash and splutter amazingly. Add the seasoning and herbs. Cover closely and cook over very low heat until the rice has absorbed all the liquid, about 20 minutes. While the rice is cooking, fry the ground meat in a separate skillet, stirring constantly until the pink color is gone. When both are cooked, combine rice and meat.

Select large firm vegetables, tomatoes, peppers, zucchini

and/or eggplant. Cut off the tops of the vegetables, saving them to use later as lids. Scoop out the insides, being careful to keep the skins intact. Fill with the prepared stuffing, replace the tops and stand them side by side in a pan. Pour in enough stock to reach half-way up the vegetables. Cover the pan and cook over a low flame until the vegetables are quite tender, about 40 minutes. Lift the Dolmas carefully from the stock and arrange on a serving platter.

The Turks invariably serve a yogurt sauce with Dolmas. It is made by diluting yogurt with some of the stock left in the pan. About 3 tablespoons stock to a cup of yogurt.

QUICHE LORRAINE

A specially delicious onion tart which serves equally well as a first course at dinner or as the main course at supper or luncheon.

1 nine inch pie shell, partially baked	2 tablespoons butter
3 slices baked ham	4 eggs
2 large onions, sliced fine	Salt and pepper
⅓ pound Swiss cheese cut into strips	Dash nutmeg
	2 cups milk, heated

Cut up the ham into bite size pieces and scatter them over the partially baked pie crust. Sauté the sliced onions in butter until tender but not brown. Spread them over the ham. Cover with the Swiss cheese. Heat milk just till skin forms on top. Now make a custard by beating the eggs with a dash of salt, pepper and nutmeg and gradually blending in the warm milk. Continue to stir the mixture constantly over low heat until the custard begins to thicken. Pour it over the ham and onions in the pie shell. Bake the Quiche at 375° for 40 minutes or until the custard is set and golden on top. Serve piping hot, directly from the pan.

The ham, onions and cheese may be arranged in the pie shell and the custard cooked long in advance, thus leaving only the combining and baking for the last minute.

Fish

PLEASANT surprises are in store for you if you are of the school that says of fish recipes with more than three ingredients, "Oh, it's too complicated, it's so much easier to fry fish." Frying is actually the most difficult method of preparing fish. And it is only for a few very delicately flavored fish that it is the best method. Most fish are easier to prepare and profit in flavor by a little dressing up.

Any fish to be good must be fresh. If you are fortunate enough to catch or to be able to buy fresh trout or dover sole, by all means pan fry or sauté it, being certain to use either a vegetable shortening or clarified butter to keep the fish from sticking to the pan or getting the soft milky consistency which butter tends to give it. Fry the fish slowly over a low flame to prevent its drying on the outside before the inside is cooked. And never, never pierce the fish with a fork to test for doneness as this will allow the juices and consequently the flavor to seep out. To test, gently lift a section with a toothpick. If the fish is flaky and the same color throughout, it is done.

The simplest and surest method for cooking most fish is poaching in the oven. Lay the fillets, slices or the whole fish in a shallow greased pan and cover with a court bouillon or with wine or fish broth. It often helps the flavor to add a bouquet garni to the pan. Cover the pan and bake in a 350° oven until done, basting frequently if the fish is large and not submerged in the liquid. After the fish is done, remove it to a platter. Pour the liquid into a pan and reduce it to whatever amount you need to prepare a sauce; that is, boil it down to the required amount. To prepare a bouquet garni, tie together sprigs of thyme, parsley, bay leaf, tarragon or rosemary, or any of your favorite herbs. If you use dried herbs you can place a pinch of each in a small piece of cheesecloth, gather the four corners together and tie them securely with a piece of fine string. To make a fish stock, put into a saucepan 1 quart of water, 1 pound inexpensive white fish and whatever heads and trimmings of fish you have on hand, 1 tablespoon salt, 2 sliced carrots, 2 sliced onions and a bouquet garni. Cover the pan closely and simmer for 45 minutes. Strain through a fine sieve and use as directed. Part of the water may be replaced by white wine.

If you wish to broil fish, remember to keep it at least 6 inches from the flame or electric coil and to baste it frequently, as fish has a tendency to become dry when broiled. Steak fish lends itself well to broiling if the above precautions are taken, particularly swordfish, salmon, halibut, sturgeon, white fish and sea bass. Perch, mackerel and other smaller fish can successfully be broiled, whole or split, but are better if poached.

Large fish are good baked, especially so since the advent of aluminium foil which makes it easy to prevent the fish from drying out. Wrap the whole fish well in aluminium foil, bake as directed, and it will come out with all the juices and flavor intact.

COD IN SAVORY CARROT SAUCE

Cod is a simple fish that is usually kept in the "all right to serve the family" category. It has surprising possibilities, however, and takes to party dress very well.

2 pounds cod	1½ cups white wine
Olive oil for frying	¼ cup brandy
¼ cup butter or margarine	½ cup water
4 large carrots, grated	1 tablespoon tomato paste
2 cloves garlic, finely chopped	1 teaspoon paprika
1 large onion, finely chopped	Salt and pepper to taste

Cut the cod into serving pieces. Heat the oil and fry the cod until brown, remove from the pan and drain well. Pour out the left over oil. Melt the butter in the pan and add the grated carrots, chopped onion and garlic and sauté until brown. Pour on the wine, brandy and water. Stir in the tomato paste and seasonings. Cover the pan and simmer for 30 minutes over low heat. Put the fish into the sauce and continue to simmer for 20 minutes. If the sauce has not reduced to the correct consistency for serving, thicken by adding a little cornstarch mixed with a little cold water and cooking for a few minutes.

SAVORY CODFISH

The inexpensive and plentiful codfish can be delicious if a little thought is given to its preparation.

6 one inch thick slices codfish	1 teaspoon tarragon, finely chopped
Salt and pepper	1 cup dry white wine
2 teaspoons shallot, finely chopped or spring onion	2 slices lemon
2 teaspoons parsley, finely chopped	3 tablespoons butter
2 teaspoons chives, finely chopped	3 tablespoons coarse bread or cracker crumbs

Place the cod slices in a well greased baking dish and season with salt and pepper. Mix all the chopped herbs together and spread them on the cod. Pour on the wine and place the lemon slices in the dish. Dot the surface with butter and cover closely. Bake at 400° for 25 minutes. Remove the cover and bake for another 5 minutes. Place the fish on a serving platter and set aside to keep warm. Pour the liquid from the baking dish into a sauce pan, add the crumbs and bring the mixture to a boil. Lower heat and simmer for 3 or 4 minutes. Pour the sauce over the fish and serve.

SCALLOPED FISH

This is a good way to use up the left over cooked cod or other cooked fish.

1 tablespoon flour	1 cup grated cheese
2 cups milk	2 cups fish, baked and flaked
1 well beaten egg	1 cup dry bread crumbs
Salt to taste	Butter to dot top
¼ teaspoon paprika	

Combine the flour, milk and beaten egg in a sauce pan and cook over low heat, stirring until thick. Season with salt and paprika. Grease a baking dish. Place in it half of the fish, cover it with half of the sauce and half of the grated cheese. Repeat the process. Cover the top with the bread crumbs and dot generously with butter. Cover the dish and bake at 375° for 15 minutes. Uncover it and continue to bake until the crumbs are crisp and golden, about 15 minutes.

SCALLOPS WITH OYSTERS

1½ pounds scallops	1 cup sliced mushrooms
⅔ cup white wine	¼ cup butter
Bouquet of herbs (thyme, bay leaf, marjoram and parsley)	1 tablespoon flour
	½ cup cream
Salt and pepper to taste	1 egg yolk
12 oysters	½ cup grated cheese

Put the scallops in a pan with the wine, herb bouquet, salt and pepper. Bring to a boil, reduce the heat and simmer for 5 minutes. Remove the scallops from the stock, and dice them into bite size pieces and set aside to keep warm. Remove the oysters from the shells. Put them into the stock and bring to a boil. Remove the oysters from the stock, add to the sliced scallops to keep warm. Sauté the mushrooms in a little of the butter in a covered pan until they are tender, about 4 minutes. Add them to the scallops and oysters, reserving the liquid that has gathered in the pan.

Now melt the remaining butter in a pan and stir in the flour until smooth. Add the drop of liquid from the mushrooms. Boil the stock in which scallops were cooked until it is reduced to $\frac{1}{2}$ cup and gradually add it to the cream mixed with the egg yolk. Gradually stir this into the flour mixture in the pan. Simmer for a minute or two and mix it into the scallops, oysters and mushrooms. Fill individual ramekins or shells or one large shallow serving dish. Sprinkle the top with grated cheese and brown quickly under the broiler or grill.

BAKED HALIBUT NASSAU

3 tablespoons bacon drippings	1 cup cooked ham, diced small
1 teaspoon chopped parsley	Salt and pepper to taste
1 teaspoon chopped green pepper	3 pound piece of halibut or 6
1 tablespoon chopped onion	halibut steaks 1 inch thick
2 tablespoons flour	Juice of 1 large lemon
1 cup hot milk	3 tablespoons grated yellow cheese
1 cup hot light cream	

Sauté the chopped parsley, green pepper and onion in the bacon drippings until soft. Sprinkle with the flour and blend well. Gradually stir in the hot milk and cream and continue stirring until the mixture thickens. Add the diced ham and the salt and pepper. Pour this sauce into a greased baking dish and place the halibut over it. Pour the lemon juice over the fish, cover the dish closely with a piece of aluminium foil. Bake at 375° for 25 minutes. Remove the aluminium foil, sprinkle the fish with the grated cheese and continue to bake until the cheese is brown.

RED SNAPPER BAKED IN TOMATO SAUCE

This savory sauce is equally good when used to bake other large fish or thick fish steaks.

3 pound red snapper, cleaned and prepared for cooking	3 cups canned tomatoes
Salt and pepper	1 tablespoon Worcestershire sauce
Flour for dredging	1 tablespoon catsup
⅓ cup butter or margarine	½ teaspoon chili powder
1 large onion, finely chopped	½ lemon, sliced
2 cups chopped celery	1 bay leaf
2 tablespoons finely chopped green pepper	1 clove garlic, finely chopped
	1 teaspoon salt

Season the fish with salt and pepper and dredge it with flour. Melt the butter in a pan, add the onion, celery and green pepper and sauté until tender. Add the other ingredients and simmer for 15 minutes. Press the sauce through a fine sieve. Place the fish in a greased baking dish, pour the sauce over it and bake, covered, at 350° for 45 minutes.

MACKEREL BROILED WITH
ANCHOVY BUTTER

Mackerel is a fish about which people have strong feelings. Some like it very much, some can't abide it. The former will go into raptures about this method of serving it, and the latter will find to their surprise that mackerel is edible after all.

2½ to 3 pounds mackerel	½ cup butter
Salt and pepper	2 teaspoons anchovy paste
4 tablespoons melted butter or	½ teaspoon onion juice
olive oil	1 teaspoon lemon juice

Split and bone the mackerel, place it skin side down in a well greased pan and season with salt and pepper. Brush it liberally with olive oil or butter. Broil 6 inches from the heat source on one side only until it is tender and flakes when tested with a toothpick. While broiling, baste it frequently with the drippings. Remove the mackerel to a serving platter and spread it with the anchovy butter, made by creaming together the butter, anchovy paste, onion juice and lemon juice.

SKATE IN CHEESE SAUCE

Fluke may be substituted for the skate in this recipe. Once you have tried these fish in other than their ordinary dress of "rolled in crumbs and fried", you will be experimenting with other ways of presenting them.

2 pounds skate	1 bay leaf
2 tablespoons butter	⅛ teaspoon thyme
3 tablespoons flour	1 onion, sliced
1½ cups milk	Salt and pepper to taste
1 clove garlic	½ cup grated Swiss cheese

Cut the fish into serving pieces. Melt 1 tablespoon butter in a sauce pan. Blend in 2 tablespoons flour and gradually stir in the milk, blending until smooth. Bring the sauce to a boil. Add the garlic, bay leaf, thyme, onion slices and salt and pepper. Put the skate into this mixture and simmer until tender, about 20 minutes. Remove the skate to an ovenproof dish, strain the liquid through a sieve, return to pan and thicken it with 1 tablespoon butter mixed with 1 tablespoon flour. Pour the thickened sauce over the skate. Cover with the grated cheese. Brown the top quickly under the broiler and serve immediately.

BAKED FISH CREOLE

Any fish which lends itself to baking will take kindly to this recipe. It is, however, particularly good with cod.

A 5 to 6 pound fish	4 cups water
4 large onions, chopped	3 sprigs parsley
4 tablespoons shortening	1 sprig thyme
2 cups soaked bread	1 bay leaf
Salt and pepper	2 cups chopped celery
1 clove garlic, chopped	4 tablespoons shortening
2½ cups canned tomatoes	1 whole clove

To prepare the stuffing, fry half the onions in 3 tablespoons shortening until brown. Add the bread that has been soaked in water and squeezed. Mix well together and fry, stirring, for 10 minutes. Season with salt and pepper and set aside to cool. Rub the inside of the fish with a mixture of 1 teaspoon salt, ½ teaspoon pepper and 1 tablespoon fat or shortening. Stuff the fish and place in a long baking pan. Bake at 450° for 30 minutes. Pour over the following sauce and bake for another 30 minutes at 350°.

To prepare the sauce, fry the remaining onions and the chopped garlic in the remaining shortening until brown. Add the tomatoes, water, clove, parsley, bay leaf, thyme and celery. Season with salt and pepper and simmer for 10 minutes. Pour over the fish and continue to bake as directed above.

SOLE, THE FISH OF MANY POSSIBILITIES

An entire book could be written on ways to present this elegant and delicious fish. Fortunately an entire book is not necessary, for once you have tried two or three recipes you will be able to make up others as you go along. Sole is very good when sautéed slowly until tender and served with melted butter and lemon juice. This method is truly simplicity *par excellence.* However, if you want just a bit of a difference you can sprinkle the sole with blanched, sliced and sautéed almonds just before serving. Sauté the sliced almonds just to the point where they take on a golden color.

The more elaborate ways of preparing sole all start out with more or less the same step, poaching in the oven, in a court-bouillon, fish stock, wine or a combination of two or three of these. From there, you can add an endless variety of ingredients to make the final product. After the fish is tender, remove to an ovenproof dish and keep warm while you make the sauce. Strain the liquid into a pan and proceed from there according to your whims that day. You may merely add cream and thicken the whole with egg yolks or flour. You may want to add sautéed mushrooms to the sauce, or grated cheese, or perhaps white grapes which you have first blanched with boiling water and peeled. Or you can arrange a mixture of other seafood around the sole before covering with the thickened sauce. Your fancy may be pleased by adding a cup of cooked shrimp to the sauce before pouring it over the fillets of sole. Another simple variation is to arrange the fillets on a bed of spinach which you have cooked, puréed and mixed with either a little heavy cream or sour cream. Pour the sauce over all and sprinkle liberally with Parmesan cheese. And so you can go on and on. I will give here a few detailed recipes to demonstrate the above. Flounder may be substituted for the sole in any recipe.

SOLE IN WINE AND CREAM

2 pounds fillet of sole	3 tablespoons butter
Juice of 1 lemon	2 tablespoons flour
2 sprigs tarragon	1 cup heavy cream
2 cloves garlic, pressed or	2 tablespoons chopped parsley
minced	Salt and pepper to taste
2 cups dry white wine	

Dip the fillets in the lemon juice and pat dry with a paper towel or cheesecloth. Lay the fillets in a greased ovenproof dish. Sprinkle the garlic and tarragon on the fish and pour on the white wine. Bake at 375° for 15 minutes. Remove the fillets to a warm serving dish and set aside to keep warm. Melt the butter in a pan, blend in the flour, gradually add the cream and 1½ cups of liquid from the sole. Bring to a boil, lower the heat and simmer until the sauce is the consistency of thick cream. Add the parsley, salt and pepper and pour over the sole. Serve immediately.

SOLE MORNAY

2 pounds fillet of sole for six	1 small onion, sliced
servings	1 clove garlic
Juice of 1 lemon	½ cup butter or margarine
¼ cup water	2 tablespoons flour
2 bay leaves	¼ cup heavy cream
⅛ teaspoon thyme	Salt and pepper
1 cup milk	½ cup grated Parmesan cheese

Wash and dry the fillets. Place them in a greased ovenproof dish. Add the lemon juice, water, bay leaves and thyme. Poach in a 375° oven for 15 minutes. Put the milk, onion and garlic in a pan. Bring to the boiling point. Melt the butter or margarine in a pan, blend in the flour until smooth and gradually add the hot milk from which you have removed the garlic and sliced onion. Simmer, stirring constantly, until the mixture begins to thicken. Pour in $\frac{1}{2}$ cup of the liquid from the poached sole and the heavy cream. Simmer for 2 more minutes. Season with salt and pepper. Arrange the fillets on a serving platter, pour the sauce over and sprinkle with the grated cheese. Brown the dish quickly under a hot broiler.

SOLE "128"

2 pounds fillet of sole	3 tablespoons heavy cream
$\frac{3}{4}$ cup fish stock	2 egg yolks, beaten
$\frac{3}{4}$ cup dry white wine	Salt and pepper to taste
Bouquet garni	

Arrange the fillets in an ovenproof dish. Pour over the fish stock and the wine. Add the bouquet garni, cover the dish with aluminium foil and bake in a 375° oven for 15 minutes. Remove the fillets to a serving dish. Strain the liquid from the sole into a pan and boil down to $1\frac{1}{2}$ cups. Stir together the cream and egg yolks. Add a bit of the hot mixture to the yolks and then gradually stir the egg yolks back into the hot mixture, stirring constantly over low heat until it thickens. Do not permit it to boil or the sauce will curdle. Season with salt and pepper. Pour the sauce over the sole, place under a hot broiler for a minute to glaze.

You may garnish this dish with white grapes, either as they are or blanched and peeled. Or with mushrooms, either whole or sliced, that have been sautéed in butter until tender. Or with onion slices that have been sautéed in butter until tender and golden. Or with the grated cheese of your choice, sprinkled on top and put under a hot broiler until brown. Or with almonds that have been blanched, sliced and sautéed until golden. And on and on.

LOBSTER TAIL THERMIDOR HOMESTYLE

I use the word "homestyle" to describe this recipe because it is so much less complicated than the traditional lobster thermidor. It is an excellent lobster dish and very easy to put together. Avail yourself of the convenience of making it well in advance and reheating before serving. Also this preparation lends itself very well to freezing. When ready to serve, heat the frozen tails at 375° for 5 minutes, sprinkle the tops with additional grated cheese and return to oven until top is brown, about 15 minutes.

6 eight ounce lobster tails
1½ cups thick white sauce
3 egg yolks, slightly beaten
1 cup sliced mushrooms,
    sautéed until tender or
1 three ounce can sliced mush-
    rooms, drained

1 teaspoon dry mustard
Salt and pepper to taste
1 cup grated American cheese
¼ cup sherry
1 tablespoon lemon juice
Additional grated cheese
2 tablespoons melted butter

Boil the lobster tails in salted water for 15 minutes. Drain and cool. Remove the membrane on underside with scissors, lift out the meat and cut it into bite size pieces. Stirring constantly, gradually add the white sauce to the egg yolks. Return to sauce pan and stirring constantly cook over low heat till thickened. Do not boil. Mix lobster meat, sauce, mushrooms, mustard, salt, pepper, cheese, sherry and lemon juice.

Fill shells with the mixture, sprinkle additional grated cheese on top, drizzle with melted butter, place in a 375° oven until heated all the way through and brown on top. If freezing for future use, place the filled tails on a cookie sheet and freeze. When frozen, wrap each tail in moisture proof paper or freezer wrap and return to freezer.

THICK WHITE SAUCE

2 tablespoons butter
3 tablespoons flour

1½ cups milk, scalded

Melt the butter in a sauce pan, blend in the flour. Gradually stir in the scalded milk, slowly bring to a boil and cook for 3 minutes, stirring constantly. Season with salt and pepper.

LOBSTER NANTUA

Lobster and mushrooms in a delicate sauce with a sprinkle of Swiss cheese is a dish to win any cook enthusiastic acclaim.

3 one pound lobsters
8 tablespoons melted butter
¾ cup dry white wine
¾ cup mushroom liquor
1½ cups sliced mushrooms

1 teaspoon lemon juice
2 tablespoons flour
1½ cups heavy cream
6 tablespoons grated Swiss cheese

Simmer the whole cleaned lobsters for 15 minutes in enough salted water barely to cover. Drain and put them into a heavy sauce pan with 6 tablespoons of the melted butter. Stir and turn the lobsters for 5 minutes, the object being to give the butter a strong lobster flavor. Add the wine and mushroom liquor, made by simmering the sliced mushrooms in just enough water to cover with a dash of salt and the lemon juice, for 5 minutes. Cover the pan closely and simmer over a low flame for 10 minutes. Drain the lobster, saving the liquid, and remove the meat from the shells. Slice the meat into bite size slices and arrange them in a shallow baking dish or in 6 individual dishes. Arrange the cooked mushrooms on the lobster. Set aside to keep warm.

Heat the remaining 2 tablespoons butter over a low flame

and stir in the flour. Gradually add the lobster liquid and the heavy cream, stirring constantly. Simmer for 5 minutes. Pour the sauce over the lobster and mushrooms and sprinkle the top with the grated Swiss cheese. Put under the broiler until delicately brown.

LOBSTER AMÉRICAINE

The lobster in this dish is usually served in the shell, with the sauce poured over all. Although it is delicious it is rather difficult and messy to eat, but that is a problem easily overcome. Just remove the meat from the shell before pouring on the sauce and you can enjoy the delicacy without the mess.

3 one pound lobsters	3 tablespoons tomato paste
5 tablespoons melted butter	⅛ teaspoon curry powder
4 tablespoons olive oil or cooking oil	⅛ teaspoon saffron
	⅛ teaspoon cayenne
1 small carrot, grated	2 cups dry white wine
2 shallots, finely chopped	Salt and pepper to taste
1 large onion, finely chopped	⅓ cup warm brandy
1 clove garlic, finely chopped	⅓ cup heavy cream
Bouquet garni of thyme, parsley and bay leaf	¼ cup finely chopped parsley
	¼ cup finely chopped chives
1 tablespoon beef extract	1 teaspoon finely chopped tarragon

Split lobsters in half, cut the tails and crack the claws. Cook the lobsters in a heavy deep skillet in the melted butter and oil, turning the pieces until the shells are red on all sides. Add the chopped vegetables and the bouquet garni. Cook and stir until the vegetables are slightly soft, about 5 minutes. Add the beef extract, tomato paste, curry, saffron, cayenne and the dry white wine. Season with salt and pepper. Cover and simmer for 40 minutes. Remove the lobster from the pan. Take the meat out of the shells and arrange it on a deep serving platter. Now pour the warmed brandy over the surface of the sauce and light. When the flame dies out, stir in the heavy cream. Pour the sauce over the lobster and sprinkle all over with the finely chopped parsley, chives and tarragon. Serve immediately.

SHRIMP DE JONG

A simple way to serve shrimp. But a tastier one would be hard to find.

3 pounds fresh shrimp	⅛ teaspoon finely chopped tarragon
1 teaspoon salt	1 tablespoon finely chopped parsley
1 stalk celery	⅛ teaspoon thyme
1 sliced carrot	⅔ cup butter
1 bay leaf	1¼ cups fine dry bread crumbs
2 tablespoons lemon juice	Salt and pepper to taste
1 large clove garlic, crushed	⅛ teaspoon nutmeg
⅛ teaspoon finely chopped onion	⅔ cup sherry

Simmer the shrimp in the court-bouillon for 15 minutes. To make a court-bouillon, add the salt, celery, carrot, bay leaf and lemon juice to a pan of boiling water. Drain the shrimp and remove shells and backbone.

Mix all the other ingredients together and blend thoroughly. Arrange alternate layers of the shelled shrimp and the bread crumb mixture in 6 well buttered individual shells or in one large 2 inch deep baking dish. Top off with the crumb mixture. Bake at 450° for 15 minutes. Serve immediately.

COQUILLE SAINT-JACQUES DIEPPOISE

Coquille is French for seashell. A Coquille Saint-Jacques is a seashell filled with scallops, mussels and mushrooms in a luscious creamy sauce that is one good reason for the French reputation for fine food. The recipe at first glance may seem complicated, for there are several steps involved. But each step is quite simple and fits in the whole very easily.

30 scallops	1½ dozen mussels
1 small onion, chopped	1 pound mushrooms, sliced
Pinch of thyme	4 tablespoons butter
1 bay leaf	3 cups Béchamel sauce
Salt and pepper	3 cups Duchesse potatoes
1 cup dry white wine	6 tablespoons grated sharp cheese

If you buy the scallops in the shell, steam them open, detach the white meat and wash it. In the States, scallops are usually sold already out of the shell and cleaned. Cut the scallops in bite size pieces. Place the scallops in a pan with the chopped onion, thyme, bay leaf, salt and pepper and the dry white wine. Simmer gently until the meat is tender. Steam open the mussel shells and remove the mussels. Cut each mussel into 3 pieces and place them in the pan with the scallops. Cook gently for 2 minutes. Remove the scallops and mussels from the liquor, strain the liquor to remove the onion and pour it into the Béchamel sauce. Sauté the mushrooms in butter until tender. Add the scallops and mussels along with the sautéed mushrooms to the sauce. Divide the seafood and sauce mixture among 6 large buttered coquilles. Sprinkle each with a tablespoon grated cheese. Using a pastry bag or tube, pipe the Duchesse potatoes in an inch wide frill around the edges of the shells. Bake in a 375° oven until the mixture is piping hot, the cheese melted, and the potatoes delicately browned.

BÉCHAMEL SAUCE

4 tablespoons butter	½ cup strong chicken stock or
4 tablespoons flour	bouillon
1 cup hot milk and heavy	Salt and paprika
cream (half and half)	2 egg yolks

Melt the butter, stir in the flour until well blended. Slowly stir in the hot milk and the stock. Cook over low heat and stir constantly until it is smooth and has bubbled gently for 2 minutes. Season with salt and paprika. Stir in the liquor from the scallops and mussels. Beat egg yolks slightly with a fork. Stir a little of the hot sauce into the yolks, enough to warm them and make it possible to pour. Carefully stir the warm egg mixture into the hot sauce. Do not boil.

DUCHESSE POTATOES

Peel 6 medium size potatoes, cover and boil until tender in salted water and force through a ricer or strainer. Add 3 tablespoons butter and 2 slightly beaten egg yolks. Blend well together.

Omelets

THE omelet is amazingly versatile and useful. A good omelet is as simple to prepare as a bad one, yet there can appear some pitfalls on the way to success with the omelet pan. But these are easy to overcome. Merely pay attention to every little detail, practice a bit and you will have a wonderful answer to many a meal problem, be it breakfast, lunch or dinner. You will have something delicious to serve at a minute's notice, an appetizing way to present leftovers of vegetables, fowl, fish, seafood or meat and an unparalleled extender of expensive food items. And once you have mastered the basic omelet, you can give your imagination and inventiveness free rein without fear of failure. The details that must be watched are the proper beating of eggs, the proper pan and the correct cooking heat.

The eggs must be completely blended but not have the life beaten out of them—beat briskly with a fork for $\frac{1}{2}$ minute, no more. Never use an electric blender as this does the job too thoroughly and leaves the eggs limp.

The omelet pan should have rounded sloping sides to permit egg mixture to spread when the pan is tilted and to permit the omelet to slide easily onto the serving plate when done. It is a good idea to keep a special pan for omelets. It may be of cast iron, heavy aluminium or copper. It must be the right size for the number of eggs used, not too large or the omelet will be too thin and dry, not too small or it will be too thick allowing the outside to become tough before the inside is cooked. A pan 8 or 9 inches in diameter is right for a 3 or 4 egg omelet, 10 or 12 inches for a 6 to 8 egg omelet. It is not practical to make a larger omelet. It is much better to make two omelets than to attempt one of more than 8 eggs; actually 6 eggs is the ideal size. Never wash the omelet pan—wipe it out with a paper towel after each use. If any particles should adhere, rub the surface with a little salt. When an omelet pan is new, season it before using by heating butter or oil in it and rubbing it in well. The pan will improve with use if properly treated. All this may sound like affectation, but it really makes good practical sense as you will soon discover if you add the omelet to your cooking repertoire.

The omelet must be cooked quickly and eaten immediately. Heat the pan on high heat, put in butter. When the butter begins to sizzle, *but before it becomes brown*, pour in the egg mixture, lower the heat and cook as directed.

PLAIN OMELET

6 eggs	Pinch of pepper
3 teaspoons cold water	1½ tablespoons butter
¼ teaspoon salt	

Break the eggs into a bowl, add the cold water, salt and pepper. Beat with a fork for ½ minute, or just enough to blend thoroughly. Do not overbeat or use an electric blender. Set your special pan on high heat. Add the butter and as it melts swirl the pan so that sides and bottom are completely coated. When the butter begins to sizzle, *but before it turns brown*, pour in the egg mixture. The underside will set immediately. Now reduce heat, tilt the pan slightly and with a fork or spatula, lift the outer edge and let the liquid egg flow under. Do this all around the pan until only the very center still retains some liquid. It is now ready to serve. Shake the pan gently so that the omelet will slip out onto the serving dish. If it should stick at any point, loosen it gently with a spatula. Now slide half the omelet onto a platter and with a quick turn of the wrist fold over it the rest of the omelet in the pan.

If the omelet is to be filled, the filling must always be fully prepared and ready to use before you prepare the omelet.

To fill the omelet, put in the filling while the omelet is still in the pan, placing the filling on the half of the omelet that will first slide out onto the platter; then the second half will cover it as you turn it out of the pan. When used as a filling, many leftovers are more tasty combined with a seasoned cream sauce or other sauce of your taste. But take care that the sauce should not be so thin that the filling runs out. If filling with cheese, place slices of cheese or the grated or chopped cheese on the omelet as soon as the outer edges are set, giving it time to melt while the omelet is cooking. The leftovers or food that you wish to extend may be stirred directly into the egg mixture and then cooked as a plain omelet, giving quite a different but equally delicious product.

Suggested variations for omelets:

Leftover vegetables such as cooked asparagus, green peas, artichoke bottoms, green beans and carrots.

Seafood such as shrimp, crabmeat, lobster and clams.

Chicken livers sautéed in butter with minced onion until done and chopped fine.

Spinach cooked until tender, puréed with a blender or put through a sieve, mixed with a bit of minced onion and bound together with a few tablespoons of sour cream, 3 tablespoons cream to a cup of spinach.

Mushrooms sliced and sautéed in butter until tender. These are best if stirred into the egg mixture before it is cooked. If used as a filling, they should be bound together with a little Béchamel sauce or sour cream.

Fine herbs, 3 tablespoons fresh herbs chopped fine, parsley, basil and chives are good, but you can use any combination of your favourite herbs. Stir into the eggs before cooking.

Leftover meat, fish or poultry, diced or minced, may be stirred directly into the egg mixture. In this case you may want to pour a sauce over the omelet when serving it. Tomato sauce is good with a meat or fish omelet; mushroom or a seasoned Béchamel sauce with a chicken, turkey or meat omelet. If you prefer to use the leftovers in a filling, they are better if bound together with a sauce, or in the case of meat with some of the meat gravy. Chopped chives or minced onion in the sauce or gravy enlivens the dish.

CLAM OMELET

6 egg omelet (page 62)	1 tablespoon chopped chives or
1 cup drained, canned, minced	grated onion
clams	Salt and pepper to taste
1 tablespoon butter	½ cup Sauce Normande

Heat the drained, minced clams with the butter, chives and seasoning. Stir in ¼ cup Sauce Normande. Make the omelet and before folding the omelet onto a platter, spread with the clam mixture. Pour the remainder of the Sauce Normande on top and serve.

SAUCE NORMANDE

2 teaspoons flour	½ teaspoon lemon juice
2 teaspoons melted butter	4 tablespoons dry white wine
Pinch of nutmeg	½ cup heavy cream
⅛ teaspoon salt and pepper	

Blend the flour into the melted butter, add the seasoning and slowly stir in the lemon juice, wine and cream. Stirring constantly over low heat cook until thickened.

CREAMED CRABMEAT OMELET

6 egg omelet (page 62)
1 cup cooked flaked crabmeat
2 tablespoons butter
Salt and pepper to taste

1 teaspoon flour
⅓ cup cream
2 tablespoons sherry

Heat the crabmeat in the butter and season with salt and pepper. Sprinkle on and blend in the flour. Slowly stir in the cream and sherry. Simmer for 2 minutes. Prepare the omelet, fill with crabmeat mixture and serve immediately.

MEAT OMELET MORNAY

6 egg omelet (page 62)
½ cup ground cooked ham
½ cup ground cooked chicken
1 tablespoon butter
1 tablespoon flour

Salt and pepper
¼ cup cream
¼ cup chicken stock
Mornay sauce
Grated Parmesan cheese

Mix the ham and chicken together. Other cooked meats may be substituted. Melt the butter in a small skillet and blend in the flour. Gradually stir in the cream and stock. Season. Simmer until thickened and combine with the ground meat. Make the omelet, fill with the meat mixture and fold out onto a platter. Pour the Mornay sauce over the omelet, sprinkle the top with the cheese and brown quickly under a hot broiler.

EASY MORNAY SAUCE

Melt 1 tablespoon butter, blend in 1½ teaspoons flour, gradually stir in ½ cup cream. Season with salt and pepper. Add 1 tablespoon grated Swiss cheese. Simmer until smooth and thickened.

SAVORY TOMATO OMELET

6 egg omelet (page 62)
3 medium sized tomatoes
1 tablespoon butter
Salt and pepper to taste

Pinch nutmeg
1 tablespoon chopped parsley
¼ teaspoon chopped basil or
  marjoram

Peel the tomatoes and cut in half, remove the seeds if you object to them. Heat the butter in a small skillet and cook the tomatoes until soft. Season with salt, pepper and nutmeg. Sprinkle on the herbs. Make omelet and fill with tomato mixture.

CHICKEN LIVER OMELET DE LUXE

6 egg omelet (page 62)
1 tablespoon butter
1 teaspoon chopped parsley
¼ teaspoon chopped chervil
¼ teaspoon chopped chives or
  scallion tops
1 clove garlic, minced

1 cup chopped cooked chicken
  livers
½ cup diced crisp bacon
2 tablespoons grated Swiss cheese
2 tablespoons cream
Grated Parmesan cheese

Melt the butter in a small skillet, add chervil, chives, the garlic and stir over low heat for 2 minutes. Add the chicken livers and stir until they begin to brown. Add the bacon and Swiss cheese and gradually stir in the cream. Make omelet and fill with chicken liver mixture. Sprinkle the top lightly with grated Parmesan cheese.

BRANDIED LOBSTER OMELET

6 egg omelet (page 62)	Salt and pepper to taste
1 tablespoon butter	1 cup diced cooked lobster meat
1 tablespoon flour	½ cup thinly sliced mushrooms
1 cup light cream	1 tablespoon brandy
2 tablespoons lobster butter or	Grated Parmesan cheese
1 teaspoon lobster paste	

Melt the butter in a small sauce pan, blend in the flour, gradually stir in the cream and simmer until smooth and thickened. Stir in the lobster butter or paste. The paste can be purchased in small jars; the butter can be made as directed below. Season to taste and add the lobster meat and mushrooms. Stir in the brandy. Make the omelet, fill with two-thirds of the lobster mixture and fold out onto a platter. Pour the rest of the mixture over the top, sprinkle generously with grated Parmesan cheese and brown quickly under a hot broiler.

Another excellent lobster omelet can be made with leftover or fresh Lobster Newburg or Thermidor.

LOBSTER BUTTER

For every ¼ cup of crushed shells use 1½ tablespoons butter and 1 teaspoon water. Simmer crushed lobster shells with butter and water for 10 minutes. Pour through a fine sieve placed over a bowl. Then pour a little boiling water over the shells to remove all the butter from them. Place the liquid in the refrigerator to chill. The butter will rise to the top and harden and can be removed for immediate use or can be packed in a jar, covered and stored for later use.

SUPPER HAM AND EGGS

6 thin slices ham	12 tablespoons cream
6 slices Swiss cheese	Salt and pepper to taste
6 eggs	

Cut ham slices into squares like a slice of bread. Place the ham slices side by side in a shallow baking dish and cover each slice with a slice of cheese. Gently break an egg atop each slice of cheese, season with salt and pepper and pour 2 tablespoons of cream over each egg. Bake at 375° until the eggs are set, about 15 minutes. Serve with toast or hot French bread and a big tossed salad.

EGGS FLORENTINE

Not really an omelet, but too good a classic egg dish to omit.

2 cups creamed spinach	Salt and pepper
Grated Parmesan cheese	Béchamel sauce
6 eggs	

Spread the creamed spinach in a shallow baking dish, about 2 inches deep. Sprinkle it with grated Parmesan cheese. Press 6 hollows into the spinach, and into each hollow break an egg. Season with salt and pepper and sprinkle generously with Parmesan cheese. Cover the entire dish with Béchamel sauce. Place the dish in a pan of hot water in a 350° oven for about 15 minutes or until the eggs are set.

BÉCHAMEL SAUCE

Melt 2 tablespoons butter, blend in 2 tablespoons flour. Stir in slowly $\frac{1}{2}$ cup milk and $\frac{1}{2}$ cup strong beef stock. Stirring constantly, cook over low heat until smooth and thickened. Beat 1 egg yolk slightly, slowly stir a little of the hot mixture and then carefully add this heated egg mixture to the hot sauce, stirring constantly. Remove from heat.

Vegetables

A GOOD menu always offers an appetite stimulating variety of colors, flavors and textures—carefully blending and contrasting the bland and sharp, the crisp and soft, the bright and pale qualities of the various foods. Vegetables are particularly valuable in achieving these desired effects. Properly prepared, they offer endless possibilities for your main course embellishment.

As a general rule, it is preferable to serve vegetables plain; that is, cooked to just the right degree of doneness and seasoned with salt, pepper and butter. Your sauces and fancy dressing up should in most cases be reserved for your main dish. To say the vegetables should usually be served plain does not, however, mean that they be prepared without care. Improperly prepared vegetables have ruined many meals. There are two cardinal rules for preparing vegetables: never, never, never overcook, and never serve swimming in water. Most people who know and care about food prefer their vegetables cooked only until they are just barely done. They should be taken from the heat and drained well before they lose firm shape.

However, to every general rule there are exceptions, and occasionally, if you have a plain main dish, you will want a new and different version of the vegetables to accompany it. There are many simple and easy ways to dress up vegetables, little additions to the plain dress of seasoning and butter, to revive

interest in a vegetable for which your taste has grown jaded.
If the dressing up becomes elaborate and rich, you then have
an entrée which is fine for luncheon, supper or for a first
course at dinner. It is a good rule never to serve a vegetable in
a highly seasoned sauce as an accompaniment to a main course
with a rich sauce.

Wash vegetables well but do not soak them in water for any
length of time. If a vegetable is a little wilted, a few minutes in
ice cold water will revive it. Vegetables such as broccoli,
asparagus, artichokes and brussel sprouts must be submerged
in water for a few minutes in order to float out the dirt and
insects that sometimes settle in them. Washing under running
water will not thoroughly clean these leafy and stemmed
vegetables. Store vegetables in a hydrater or covered container
in the refrigerator to keep them fresh.

Cook all vegetables in a covered pan as quickly as possible
in as little boiling salted water as possible. Just $\frac{1}{4}$ inch depth
of water is a good starting rule—you will be able to adjust
amounts as your experience increases. Cook only until they
are barely tender. Drain them immediately to prevent loss
of color and firmness. The rapid boiling helps retain color and
the small quantity of water prevents all the vitamins from seep-
ing out into a broth. Melt butter in a pan, 1 tablespoon of
butter per cup of vegetables, return vegetables to pan, cover
and shake gently until butter is evenly distributed. Serve
immediately, never insult your guests or family with cold
vegetables.

Corn on the cob is cooked in just barely enough water to
cover, seasoned with 1 tablespoon of sugar and simmered for
only 5 minutes.

Young whole tender green beans are delicious when cooked
until barely tender and served with melted (drawn) butter. If
the beans are larger—that is, if picked later in the season or of a
larger variety—they are better if cut French style, sliced in long
slivers, and then cooked as above. For a change you can point

up beans by the mere addition of almonds that have been blanched, sliced and sautéed in butter until they begin to turn golden. Use 1 tablespoon of sliced sautéed almonds to each cup of beans and toss them together with a fork. To blanch almonds pour boiling water over them and boil for $\frac{1}{2}$ minute, drain and slip off the skins.

Another interesting variation is to mix through the beans mushrooms that have been sliced and sautéed in butter in a covered pan for 4 minutes or until tender.

Broccoli, brussel sprouts and cauliflower are beautifully complemented with a simple topping of buttered bread crumbs or cheese sauce. To make the buttered crumbs, roll very dry bread until fine or put it through a food chopper. Melt 2 tablespoons of butter for each cup of vegetables. When the butter begins to bubble, add to the pan 2 tablespoons of crumbs for each tablespoon of butter. Toss together with a fork until the crumbs are well saturated with butter. Arrange the vegetables on a serving dish and cover with the crumbs. To make cheese sauce, place 2 tablespoons of yellow processed cheese for each cup of vegetables in the top of a double boiler. Add a teaspoon or so of cream to the pan and place over boiling water until the cheese is melted. Pour over the vegetables just before serving.

Sour cream just as it comes from the container makes a welcome and easy change from butter as a topping for any of the green vegetables.

Asparagus and broccoli go well with Hollandaise sauce. If young and tender, asparagus is best with just melted butter or butter and lemon juice, but if the asparagus is slightly bigger (although still good with just butter) sautéed mushrooms over which you have sprinkled a tablespoon of sherry make a tasty topping and camouflages the age of the asparagus.

Carrots and small white onions are delicious when glazed. Cook the vegetables until barely tender, drain and allow to dry. Melt in a pan $1\frac{1}{2}$ tablespoons of butter for each cup of vegetables, add 1 teaspoon of sugar for each 1½ tablespoons of butter. When sugar is dissolved and begins to bubble, add the vegetables and turn them with a fork until well coated with the butter and sugar mixture. Cook on a very low flame, stirring occasionally for 5 minutes.

More detailed recipes follow.

DUTCH POTATO PUFFS

Mounds of golden goodness that make a welcome addition to any meal be it quite modest or very splendid.

6 medium sized potatoes	3 tablespoons chopped parsley
2 tablespoons flour	1 tablespoon melted butter
2 beaten eggs	Salt, pepper and nutmeg to taste
1 clove garlic, crushed	

Peel, boil and mash the potatoes. Blend in the other ingredients and mix thoroughly together. Place heaped tablespoons of the mixture on a flat greased baking dish. Bake at 350° for 15 minutes. Now pop them under a hot broiler or grill just long enough to brown the tops. Pour a little melted butter over the puffs and serve immediately.

BOILED POTATOES AND ONIONS

6 medium sized potatoes	Salt and pepper
6 small onions	¼ teaspoon vinegar
2 tablespoons butter	¼ teaspoon flour

Boil the potatoes until tender, slice into a serving dish and keep warm until the onions are ready. Slice the onions thinly and sauté in butter until tender and begin to turn brown. Sprinkle with salt, pepper, flour and vinegar, mix well and simmer for

10 minutes. Spread the onions over the hot sliced potatoes and serve.

POTATO PANCAKES

These crispy potato pancakes make a welcome change from pan fried potatoes and go well with all those dishes that call for fried potatoes.

2 cups raw grated potatoes	Salt and pepper to taste
1 egg, slightly beaten	2 tablespoons flour
1 onion, grated fine	

Mix all ingredients together. Fry in a heavy skillet in hot oil about ⅛ inch deep until golden brown on both sides. Drain on absorbent paper towel. May be served with apple sauce or a topping of sour cream.

SCALLOPED POTATOES AND ONIONS

8 medium sized potatoes	Salt and pepper
4 medium sized onions	3 tablespoons flour
½ pound sharp cheese, grated	Milk to cover

Slice the potatoes into thin even slices. Chop the onions coarsely. Arrange the potatoes, onions and grated cheese in alternate layers in a greased baking dish, seasoning each layer with salt and pepper and sprinkling with flour. Pour milk over all to cover. Cover the baking dish and bake at 350° for 1½ to 2 hours, until the potatoes are very tender and the milk is reduced and thickened. This dish is equally good the second day. Merely reheat.

POTATO CHEESE PUFF

This tasty golden potato dish will please all those who have grown tired of potatoes in their ordinary dress. Here, too, is an appropriate luncheon main course.

8 medium potatoes	½ teaspoon salt
⅛ cup butter	1 large onion, minced fine
1½ cups grated sharp yellow cheese	¼ teaspoon celery salt
¾ cup milk	⅛ teaspoon pepper
	2 eggs, well beaten

Boil the potatoes until tender, drain and mash well. Add the butter, grated cheese, milk, salt, onion, celery salt and pepper and stir over low heat until cheese and butter are melted. Gradually fold in the beaten eggs. Turn the mixture into a greased casserole and bake, uncovered, at 375° for 45 minutes, until the potatoes are puffy and brown. Bring the casserole directly from the oven to the table.

POTATO FRITTERS

2 cups hot mashed or riced potatoes	4 eggs, well beaten
2 tablespoons cream	Salt and pepper to taste
2 tablespoons white wine	½ cup flour

Add the cream, wine and seasoning to the hot mashed potatoes. Stir in the beaten eggs, place the mixing bowl in a pan of ice water and beat until the mixture is cold. Beat in the flour. Drop heaped tablespoonsful into hot deep fat. Fry until golden and puffy.

POTATO NESTS

These delightfully crusty nests are excellent filled with creamed meat or vegetables.

2 cups mashed potatoes	1 egg, well beaten
Salt and pepper to taste	1 medium onion, minced fine
1 tablespoon cream	Melted butter

Mix all the ingredients together. Form into balls and press down center to form nests. Place in greased muffin pans and brush surface with melted butter. Sprinkle with dry fine bread crumbs and bake at 375° for 30 minutes. To serve, fill with creamed meat, fish or vegetables.

TOMATOES PROVENÇALE

These tomatoes are particularly good with steak or roast beef. Or try them with ground beef patties, egg or cheese dishes.

6 large firm tomatoes	4 tablespoons olive oil
Salt and pepper	1 large clove garlic, crushed
1 cup fine dry bread crumbs	3 tablespoons finely chopped parsley

Cut the tomatoes in half, crosswise, sprinkle the cut surface with salt and pepper. Blend remaining ingredients together thoroughly and spread over each cut surface. Place 3 inches from heat source under broiler set at low heat and broil for 10 minutes or until nicely brown on top and the tomato is tender.

GRILLED TOMATOES AND ONIONS

3 large sweet onions	2 tablespoons brown sugar
3 large firm tomatoes	3 tablespoons butter
Salt, pepper and paprika	

Cut the onions crosswise in $\frac{1}{2}$ inch slices. Drop them into boiling salted water and cook rapidly for 7 minutes. Drain well. Cut the tomatoes crosswise into 1 inch slices, arrange them alternately with the onion slices in a well greased large flat baking dish. Season the onion slices with salt and pepper and the tomatoes with salt, paprika and the brown sugar. Dot the onions and tomatoes with butter. Bake at 350° for 20 minutes, then place under a hot broiler until well browned and bubbly. Serve them stacked in alternate layers.

CANDIED TOMATOES

Canned or fresh tomatoes may be used with equal success in this dish which goes so very well with cheese omelets or soufflés, or as a topping for boiled rice to accompany chicken or a plain meat roast.

2 tablespoons butter	1 teaspoon salt
$\frac{1}{4}$ cup finely chopped onion	6 tablespoons brown sugar
1 quart canned tomatoes or 6 large fresh peeled tomatoes	

Sauté the onion in the butter until tender and brown. Add the tomatoes, salt and brown sugar. If using fresh tomatoes, add $\frac{1}{3}$ cup water to the pan and cook covered until the tomatoes form their own juice. Cook very, very slowly over a low flame until the juice has become thick and slightly sticky. Note: to peel fresh tomatoes plunge them into boiling water, continue boiling for 1 minute or until the skins crack. Pour off boiling water, plunge into cold water, remove from water and remove skins.

GREEN BEANS À LA CRÈME

A truly delicious dish that deserves to be the center of attraction at a meal. Serve it with a plain grilled or roasted meat or broiled chicken. No other sauce should conflict with the rich nutty flavour.

1 cup almonds, blanched	1 pound mushrooms, sliced
2 packages frozen French style green beans or 1 pound fresh young beans cut French style	4 tablespoons butter
	2 tablespoons flour
	2 cups heavy cream

Slice almonds and toast in oven until golden. Cook the beans until barely tender and drain. Sauté the sliced mushrooms in 2 tablespoons butter in a covered pan for 5 minutes or until tender. Melt the remaining butter in a sauce pan, blend in the flour, gradually add the heavy cream, stirring constantly and simmer until the sauce thickens. Season with salt and pepper. Toss the beans and mushrooms together, and pour the sauce over them. Fold the sauce through the mixed vegetables. Put into a serving dish and sprinkle the top with the golden almond slices.

GREEN BEANS WITH MUSTARD COATING

Particularly suited to ham or broiled chicken.

1 pound young green beans	½ cup milk
1 teaspoon dry mustard	2 teaspoons vinegar
1 tablespoon butter	Salt to taste
2 egg yolks	

Cook the beans in a small amount of boiling salted water until tender, about 10 minutes, and drain. While the beans are cooking, add the mustard and butter to the egg yolks and with a wire whisk beat the mixture until it is light and bubbly. Heat the milk and gradually add it to the egg yolk mixture. Cook the mixture in a double boiler until it is thickened, stirring constantly. Add the vinegar, salt and the beans. Continue to cook for 5 minutes.

SWEET AND SOUR BEANS

An extremely pleasant change from buttered beans and simple enough to serve with a rich or elaborate main dish.

1 pound green beans or	½ tablespoon flour
2 ten ounce packages frozen	½ cup brown sugar
beans	1 lemon cut up into very small
1 tablespoon butter	pieces

Cook the beans in a small amount of boiling salted water for 10 minutes or until tender. Drain. Mix together the butter and flour, put into a pan and stir over low heat until the roue is brown, add the brown sugar, stir until the sugar is melted. Add the lemon and continue to cook, stirring, for 2 minutes. Add the cooked beans and cook, stirring, just long enough for the beans to become hot and flavored with the sauce.

BEETS WITH ORANGE SAUCE

Simple but flavorful. Especially good served with pork roast, pork chops or broiled chicken.

2½ cups diced, cooked beets, or	2 teaspoons flour
small whole cooked beets	¾ cup orange juice
1 tablespoon butter	¼ teaspoon salt
4 tablespoons brown sugar	⅛ teaspoon paprika

Melt butter in top of double boiler. Blend in the sugar mixed with the flour. Stir in the orange juice. Stir and cook until thick. Add seasoning and beets. Continue to cook until the beets are thoroughly heated.

SPINACH RING WITH MUSHROOMS
AND EGGS

Another vegetable dish that deserves to be the center of interest at a meal.

1 cup cooked spinach (1 ten ounce package frozen spinach or 1½ pounds fresh spinach)	1 cup light cream
	3 egg yolks, beaten
	Salt and pepper to taste
3 tablespoons butter	⅛ teaspoon nutmeg
1 tablespoon chopped onion	3 egg whites, beaten until stiff
3 tablespoons flour	

Drain the cooked spinach thoroughly. Put it through a food chopper or use an electric blender to purée it very finely. Reserve. Melt the butter in a large skillet. Sauté the onion in it until tender and golden. Blend in the flour. Add the cream slowly while stirring. Cook, stirring until thickened and smooth. Stir a little of the hot mixture into the beaten egg yolks, then stirring constantly slowly pour the yolks into the hot mixture. Cook for 1 minute, stirring constantly. Add the spinach. Season to taste with salt, pepper and the nutmeg. Remove from the heat. Beat the egg whites until stiff and fold them into the spinach mixture. Turn into a well greased 8 inch mold. Set the mold in a pan of hot water. Bake at 325° for 40 minutes or until set. Invert on a serving platter and fill the center with the mushrooms and eggs which you have prepared while the spinach is baking:

2 eggs	½ cup cream
1 clove garlic	¾ cup whole milk
2 tablespoons butter	Salt to taste
1 pound sliced mushrooms	2 tablespoons chopped parsley
2 tablespoons flour	1 tablespoon lemon juice

Hard boil the eggs. While the eggs are cooking, rub a skillet with the garlic. Melt the butter in the skillet, and when it begins to bubble remove the garlic. Add the sliced mushrooms, lower the heat and cook covered until the mushrooms are tender, about 4 minutes. Sprinkle flour over the mushrooms. Slowly stir in the cream and the milk. Cook over low heat stirring until thickened. Cut each egg into quarters and add to the mushrooms. Season with salt and add the parsley and lemon juice.

SPINACH MOLD

1½ pounds washed spinach or 1 ten ounce package of frozen spinach	½ cup stock from cooking spinach
	½ cup heavy cream
4 tablespoons butter	2 eggs
Salt and pepper	2 cups croûtons
3 tablespoons flour	Butter

Place the spinach in a sauce pan with 2 tablespoons butter, the salt and pepper and cook for 5 minutes over a low flame, stirring almost constantly. The spinach will make its own juice as it cooks. Drain the spinach well, reserving the liquid. Purée the spinach by rubbing it through a sieve, putting it through a food chopper or in an electric blender. Melt the remaining 2 tablespoons butter in a pan, blend in the flour. Slowly add the liquid from the spinach and stir until the mixture thickens. Add ¼ cup of the heavy cream and bring to a boil. Cool and add to the spinach along with the beaten eggs. Salt and pepper to taste. Pour into a well greased mold, cover closely, set into a shallow pan of hot water and bake at 375° for 25 minutes. Remove from oven and water bath and let stand for 5 minutes before unmolding onto a serving platter. Fry croûtons in butter until golden. Pour the remaining ¼ cup of cream over the top and surround the mold with the golden croûtons.

G.K.—6

PURÉED SPINACH WITH SOUR CREAM

3 pounds fresh spinach or 2 ten
  ounce packages frozen spinach
1 medium onion, chopped fine

2 tablespoons butter
2 tablespoons flour
⅝ cup sour cream

Wash the spinach well. Cook in a covered pan with the minimum of water to keep the spinach from scorching, about ⅓ cup, for 5 minutes. Drain well. Purée the spinach in an electric blender, a food chopper or by rubbing through a fine strainer. Melt the butter in a skillet, add the onion and sauté until soft and golden. Add the puréed spinach. Sprinkle with flour and stir well. When spinach is piping hot, stir in the sour cream, heat thoroughly but do not permit it to boil. Serve immediately.

SPINACH SOUFFLÉ

Good as the vegetable at dinner if the main dish is not too elaborate or heavy, but even better as a luncheon or supper dish. In the latter case, double the recipe as you will want bigger servings.

4 tablespoons flour
4 tablespoons butter
1 teaspoon salt
⅛ teaspoon pepper
2 tablespoons chopped onion
2 cups milk

4 egg yolks, beaten
1½ cups cooked and finely chopped
  spinach
4 egg whites, stiffly beaten
½ cup grated cheese (optional)

Blend the butter and flour together in the top of a double boiler or in a heavy bottomed sauce pan. Add the salt, pepper and onion and allow to cook together for 3 minutes. Add the milk slowly, stirring constantly until thick and smooth. Pour a little of the hot sauce onto the beaten yolks and then stir the yolks into the sauce, continuing to stir and cook for a minute. Remove from the heat, fold in the spinach (and the cheese if desired) and the stiffly beaten egg whites. Put into a greased and floured casserole, set in a pan of hot water and place in a 325° oven for ½ hour or until firm. Serve immediately.

FRENCH PEAS

Truly delicious. Simple enough to serve with even an elaborate main dish and flavorful enough to accent the vegetable portion of the meal.

4 tablespoons butter	½ smallhead iceberg lettuce,
1 onion, finely chopped	shredded
2 pounds fresh green peas or	½ cup bouillon or stock
2 packages frozen peas	

Melt 3 tablespoons butter in the bottom of a sauce pan. Sauté the chopped onion in the butter until soft but not brown. Add the peas and shredded lettuce and the stock. If you do not have stock on hand, dissolve 1 bouillon cube in ½ cup water. Cover the pan closely and simmer on a low flame for 10 to 15 minutes or until the peas are tender. Add another tablespoon of butter and serve. If the pan becomes dry before the peas are tender, add a little stock.

PEAS, ONION AND CELERY

This recipe is a variation of French peas, just as simple and tasty.

1 medium onion, chopped fine	2 pounds fresh peas or 2 packages
3 large stalks celery, chopped fine	frozen peas
	4 tablespoons butter

Cook the onion and celery in a small amount of salted water for 5 minutes. Add the peas to the pan and continue to cook, covered, for another 5 minutes for frozen peas and 10 minutes for fresh peas. Drain the vegetables well and toss with 4 tablespoons melted butter before serving.

MUSHROOMS WITH SOUR CREAM

This is particularly good served with plain broiled steak, roast beef, ground beef patties or broiled chicken. I would not serve it with any main dish that had a sauce.

4 tablespoons butter	1 cup strong stock or bouillon
1½ pounds mushrooms, sliced	1 cup sour cream
2 tablespoons flour	

Melt the butter in a skillet, add the mushrooms and sauté, covered for 5 minutes or until tender. Sprinkle the mushrooms with flour and stir until blended. Gradually add the stock and cook, stirring, until thickened. Stir in the sour cream, heat thoroughly but do not boil.

ARTICHOKES

The subtle and succulent artichoke should receive more attention than it usually gets. Boiled until tender in a court-bouillon, drained and served with a hot lemon butter sauce for dipping each leaf, the artichoke is delicious and elegant. Hollandaise sauce or mayonnaise are also wonderful dips to try. But many unusual recipes can be developed. Here are two elaborate ones. If you try them, I am certain you will be inspired to invent another of your own.

STUFFED ARTICHOKES

3 good sized artichokes	⅔ cup stale bread crumbs
2 strips bacon	¼ cup beef stock or bouillon
¼ cup chopped mushrooms	Salt and pepper to taste
2 tablespoons finely chopped onion	⅛ teaspoon paprika
	2 tablespoons butter

Wash and trim the artichokes and remove the chokes. Cook them in boiling salted water until almost tender, about 20 minutes. Cut the bacon into bits and cook in a skillet until it begins to brown. Add the mushrooms and onion and sauté for 3 minutes. Add the bread crumbs. Moisten with the stock. Season with salt, pepper and paprika. Cut the artichokes in halves lengthwise, fill with the stuffing and arrange them in a shallow baking dish. Dot the top with butter. Cover the bottom of the dish with water and bake in a 375° oven for ½ hour, basting occasionally with a little melted butter.

ARTICHOKE BOTTOMS AU FOIE GRAS

Delicious but rich. A little goes a long way, but that little does much to point up a meal. If you wish to serve these as the main dish at luncheon or supper, prepare two or three for each serving.

1 tablespoon butter	6 bottoms of large cooked artichokes
1 tablespoon flour	or canned artichoke bottoms
1½ cups light cream	Lemon juice, salt and pepper
3 tablespoons grated Swiss cheese	6 ¼ inch slices of foie gras
Salt and pepper	6 teaspoons sherry or madeira

To prepare the Béchamel sauce, blend together the butter and flour, heat the cream and slowly stir into it the butter and flour mixture. Continue to cook and stir until mixture thickens. Season with salt and pepper. Add the grated cheese. Arrange the artichoke bottoms in a shallow greased baking dish. Sprinkle each with lemon juice, salt and pepper and place on each a slice of foie gras. Pour a teaspoon of sherry or madeira on each. Cover each with a generous portion of sauce and put into a hot, 450° oven until glazed.

HUBBARD SQUASH BAKED IN CREAM

The homely squash becomes elegant fare with a little special attention. If squash is not available, pumpkin may be used.

6 cups peeled and thinly sliced Hubbard squash	6 tablespoons sugar
Salt and pepper	1½ cups heavy cream
	1½ teaspoons cinnamon

Arrange the sliced squash in a well greased baking dish. Sprinkle it with salt and pepper and the sugar. Pour over it the heavy cream and sprinkle the top with cinnamon. Bake at 300° for 1 hour or until the squash is tender. Serve from the baking dish.

SQUASH SOUFFLÉ

This dish presents an attractive color combination and tastes just as good as it looks.

3 cups cooked or canned yellow squash	⅛ teaspoon pepper
1 tablespoon minced onion	3 tablespoons melted butter
1 teaspoon salt	3 eggs, well beaten
	2 cups cooked and buttered peas

Mash the squash well, mix it with the onion, salt, pepper and melted butter. Stir in the beaten eggs and pour into a well

greased ring mold. Place in a pan with ½ cup hot water and
bake in a 350° oven for 45 minutes. Unmold before serving
and fill the center of the mold with the peas.

PARSNIPS

Parsnips are usually associated with the country kitchen. They
store well, and in midwinter when other fresh vegetables used
to be unattainable they made their appearance. With a little
attention, they, like the homely squash, can hold their own on
any dinner table at any time of year. They are good glazed;
that is, boiled until tender, drained well and then tossed over a
low heat until well glazed in a butter and sugar mixture. Or
you can put the whole cooked parsnips in a shallow baking
dish, sprinkle them with salt, paprika and brown sugar. Dot
them generously with butter and top with dry bread crumbs.
Pour over them enough cream to cover bottom of dish and
bake at 400° until top is well browned. For parsnips "with a
difference", try this mashed ring.

MASHED PARSNIP OR SQUASH RING

8 to 10 medium sized parsnips or medium yellow squash cooked in boiling salted water until tender	1 teaspoon salt
	¼ cup butter
	2 tablespoons vinegar
	1 egg, beaten
⅛ teaspoon paprika	Minced parsley, optional

Mash the cooked parsnips or squash until you have a fine
purée. You may want to put them through a sieve or fine food
chopper. Add the seasoning, butter, vinegar and beaten egg.
Return to the sauce pan and heat thoroughly, giving the egg
time to become cooked. Turn the mixture onto a hot platter
and with a spoon and fork form it into a ring, roughening the

outer edge with the tines of the fork. Sprinkle top with minced parsley. Fill the center with a creamed vegetable if you wish.

EGGPLANT CASSEROLE

1 medium sized eggplant	½ cup chopped onion
2 tablespoons butter	1 teaspoon salt
3 tablespoons flour	1 tablespoon brown sugar
3 large tomatoes or 2 cups	1 bay leaf
canned tomatoes	1 cup fine dry bread crumbs
¼ cup chopped green pepper	2 tablespoons butter

Peel the eggplant and cut into ½ inch cubes. Cook it for 10 minutes in boiling salted water. Drain and place in a greased baking dish. Melt 2 tablespoons butter in a skillet, add the flour and stir until blended. Peel the tomatoes and chop coarsely and add to the butter along with the pepper, onion, salt, brown sugar and bay leaf. Cook for 5 minutes. Pour the sauce over the eggplant. Cover the top with the bread crumbs, dot with butter. Bake at 350° for 30 minutes.

FRIED EGGPLANT OR ZUCCHINI WITH YOGURT

The Turks have a tendency to top all vegetables and many meats with yogurt. In the case of eggplant and zucchini they are so right! And another point they are right about in treating eggplant is that they never slice, salt and weight the eggplant for hours before cooking it. This step is entirely unnecessary.

Peel and cut in ¼ inch thick slices sufficient eggplant for six servings. If you are using zucchini, it should not be peeled and should be sliced lengthwise. Dredge the slices with flour, season with salt and paprika. Cover the bottom of a large skillet with olive oil, heat the oil and sauté the eggplant slices slowly until they are tender and golden brown. Do not crowd the pan. Drain the slices on absorbent paper and keep hot in the oven. Serve piping hot with cold yogurt.

FRIED EGGPLANT OR ZUCCHINI BORDELAISE

Prepare the eggplant and zucchini slices and fry them as directed above. When all the slices are browned, set in a hot oven to keep warm. Add to the hot oil in the pan a mixture of:

1 small onion, chopped fine	2 tablespoons chopped parsley
1 clove of garlic, minced	½ cup fine dry bread crumbs

Sauté for 3 minutes being careful not to scorch. It may be necessary to add a bit more oil, but do not do so unless absolutely necessary as you do not want a greasy product. Drain the crumbs on absorbent paper and then sprinkle them over the hot eggplant or zucchini slices.

EGGPLANT AND TOMATOES AU GRATIN

1 large eggplant, sliced in ¼ inch slices	¼ cup finely chopped onion
Flour	Salt and pepper to taste
Butter	2 tablespoons flour
8 medium sized tomatoes	3 tablespoons heavy cream
3 tablespoons butter	1 cup grated Swiss cheese

Dip the eggplant slices in flour and fry in butter until tender.
Peel the tomatoes and dice coarsely. In a skillet, melt the butter and sauté the onion until golden. Add the tomatoes,

salt and pepper and continue to cook until the tomatoes are soft. Sprinkle the vegetables with the flour and stir until it thickens. Add the cream. Arrange the fried eggplant slices and the tomato mixture in alternate layers in a greased baking dish, starting with the eggplant slices and ending with the tomato mixture. Cover the top with the grated Swiss cheese and bake in a 450° oven until brown, about 10 minutes.

TURNIPS AND PEAS AU GRATIN

2 cups diced turnips, white or yellow
1 cup canned peas
1 cup medium thick white sauce

Salt and pepper to taste
⅓ cup grated cheese
⅓ cup buttered bread crumbs

Peel the turnips, cut into dice and cook in boiling salted water until tender. Drain. Add the cooked peas, white sauce and salt and pepper. Turn into a greased baking dish, top with the buttered crumbs and grated cheese. Bake at 375° for 10 minutes or until golden brown.

ZUCCHINI AND MUSHROOMS IN SOUR CREAM

1 pound mushrooms, thickly sliced
1 pound zucchini, cut in 1 inch slices
¼ cup butter

1 clove garlic
2 tablespoons butter
2 tablespoons flour
1 cup sour cream
1 teaspoon finely chopped dill

Do not peel either of the vegetables. Melt the butter in a large skillet, add the sliced mushrooms, zucchini and garlic, and sauté for 5 minutes, stirring frequently. Remove the garlic clove. Sprinkle the vegetables with the flour and continue to cook for 3 minutes. Stir in the sour cream and dill. Heat thoroughly but do not boil.

OKRA AND TOMATOES À LA NEW ORLEANS

Shades of the old South in this hearty dish that shows the true worth of the okra.

4 slices bacon cut into small
    pieces
5 cups of okra cut into thin
    slices

5 cups tomatoes cut into wedges
    or canned tomatoes
1 bay leaf
Salt and pepper to taste

In a large skillet fry the bacon pieces until they begin to become crisp. Add the sliced okra and cook until it browns. Add the peeled tomato wedges and the bay leaf. Simmer over very low heat for 3 hours. If the mixture becomes too thick and threatens to scorch, add a little tomato juice.

BAKED CABBAGE

Either you like cabbage or you don't. If you do, you will like it better this way; if you don't, perhaps even this won't convert you. But I think it will.

1 medium sized head of cabbage
3 well beaten eggs
2 tablespoons melted butter
⅔ cup light cream
¼ teaspoon salt

¼ teaspoon paprika
1 cup fine dry bread crumbs or
    1 cup grated sharp cheese
2 tablespoons butter

Cut the cabbage into thin slices, place in ½ inch boiling water, cover and cook for 10 minutes only. Drain. Place it in a greased baking dish. Combine the beaten eggs, cream, melted butter, salt and paprika; pour over the cabbage. Bake at 325° until brown, about 35 minutes. Cover the top with the dry bread crumbs, or the grated cheese, dot with 2 tablespoons butter and return to the oven until crumbs are brown or cheese is melted.

SCALLOPED CAULIFLOWER

1 medium sized head cauliflower	¼ teaspoon salt
2 tablespoons butter	1 teaspoon onion juice
1½ tablespoons flour	1 cup grated sharp cheese
1 cup hot milk	

Wash well and cut off the outer leaves and the stem from the cauliflower. Place it head up in a pan of boiling salted water about ½ inch deep. Cook covered for 15 minutes. Drain well. Separate the flowerets. Place them in a greased baking dish. Melt the butter in a pan, stir in the flour, gradually blend in the hot milk. Season with salt and onion juice. Stir in the grated cheese. Pour over the cauliflower. Bake in a 450° oven for 10 minutes or until golden brown and bubbly.

SOUTHERN STYLE CORN

¼ cup chopped onion	⅛ teaspoon pepper
¼ cup chopped green pepper	½ cup milk
2 tablespoons butter	1 egg, beaten
1 tablespoon flour	1½ cups corn niblets
1 teaspoon salt	½ cup buttered bread crumbs

Cook the onion and green pepper in butter slowly for 5 minutes. Add flour, salt and pepper and mix well. Add the milk to the beaten egg and then stir it slowly into the onion mixture. Add the corn and mix well. Place in a greased 1 quart baking dish. Cover with the buttered crumbs. Bake at 350° for 40 minutes.

LIMA BEANS AND TOMATOES
IN CASSEROLE

3 tablespoons butter
¼ cup finely chopped onion
1½ cups cooked tomatoes
Salt and pepper to taste

2 cups cooked fresh or frozen
  lima beans
½ cup fine dry bread crumbs
½ cup grated Parmesan cheese

Heat the butter in a pan and in it sauté the onion. Add the tomatoes and season to taste. Simmer for 10 minutes. Cook the lima beans in boiling salted water for 10 minutes and drain well. Mix tomatoes and limas together. Pour into a casserole, sprinkle with the bread crumbs and the Parmesan cheese. Bake at 375° for ½ hour, until the topping is well browned.

ORANGE SWEET POTATOES

6 medium sized sweet potatoes
1 cup orange juice
2 teaspoons grated orange rind
1 tablespoon cornstarch

3 tablespoons melted butter
¼ cup brown sugar
¼ cup granulated sugar

Boil the sweet potatoes until they are almost but not quite, done (about 25 minutes). Peel and cut them in half lengthwise and arrange them in a greased baking dish. Combine the other ingredients in a pan and cook, stirring, until thickened. Pour the mixture over the sweet potatoes, cover and bake at 350° for 20 minutes, uncover and bake another 15 minutes. Excellent with ham or poultry.

SWEET POTATO SOUFFLÉ

Sweet potatoes just naturally go with ham, turkey or chicken. This method of presenting them is a welcome change from the usual candied or baked sweets.

2 cups boiled, mashed sweet potatoes
½ cup hot milk
¼ cup sherry
½ cup butter
⅛ teaspoon nutmeg

½ teaspoon salt
1 teaspoon finely grated lemon rind
4 egg yolks, well beaten
4 egg whites, stiffly beaten

Measure the mashed sweet potatoes into a mixing bowl; add the hot milk, sherry and butter. Beat the mixture together until it is smooth. While beating, add the nutmeg, salt, lemon rind and well beaten egg yolks. Fold in the stiffly beaten egg whites. Turn the mixture into a greased soufflé dish and bake it at 400° for 30 minutes or until it is brown and puffy. Serve immediately upon removing from the oven.

GLORIFIED SWEET POTATOES

Southern in character, universal in appeal, these sweet potatoes will add glory to any table. Excellent with ham, Canadian bacon or turkey. Especially good at a buffet with cold sliced turkey.

6 to 8 medium sized sweet potatoes
¼ cup cream
¼ teaspoon nutmeg
2 tablespoons finely grated orange rind

¼ teaspoon powdered cloves
2 egg yolks, well beaten
½ cup brown sugar
3 tablespoons brandy
1 cup coarsely chopped salted peanuts or salted pecans

Boil sweet potatoes until tender, peel and mash. Mix together and beat until fluffy the mashed sweet potatoes, cream, nutmeg, grated orange rind, cloves and beaten egg yolks. Turn them into a buttered casserole, cover the top with the brown sugar. Sprinkle on the chopped salted peanuts or pecans and the brandy. Bake at 450° until well heated and browned on top, about 10 to 15 minutes.

Dessert Pastry

MOST American housewives limit their pastry efforts to pie crusts. It is of course true that for the typical American home the most frequently demanded pastry item from the home kitchen is the crust for a pie. And so, for those who are either hesitant about making a pie crust or who find their results something less than the flaky product aimed for, I am including here the instructions for my favorite method.

But variety is essential to good eating. No cook, who wishes to be envied and respected by those who know and appreciate a fine table, can restrict her pastry accomplishments to one item. I am therefore including recipes and methods for making other types of pastry. These will offer you a basis for creating many variations of pastry desserts. All of these are eminently qualified for your most ambitious dinner party and, once you have mastered the technique, you will even prepare them often for your family alone.

First, there is puff paste. Rare is the person interested in food who has not eaten and enjoyed it. But, unfortunately, almost equally rare is the lady who bakes it at home. Once you have tried this recipe, your regret that you had earlier limited your enjoyment of it to an occasional Napoleon in a good French restaurant will be matched by your pleasure at what you can do yourself. Next are the French *Galette* and German *Muerbe Teig* which are the European counterparts of our pie crust.

You will find these much appreciated departures from the crust commonly prepared in America. Lastly, the French *Pâté-à-choux*—or pastry used for cream puffs. This is another versatile pastry, which you will quickly discover goes far beyond the usual filling with boiled custard or whipped cream.

PIE CRUST I

The shortening should be as cold as possible. The water should be iced.

Use a pastry cloth and rolling pin cover and a pastry blender.

Most important of all, use a light hand. The dough should be handled as lightly and as little as possible. *Do not be disturbed if you are unable to pick up your crust in one piece.* You can press the edges of the pieces together in the pan and after it is baked the patches will not show. A crust that is smooth and easy to handle is likely to be tough. A pie crust may frequently look a bit messy before it is baked, yet, after baking, is so tender and flaky that it literally melts in the mouth.

For 1 two crust or 2 single crust pies:

1½ cups sifted all purpose flour (6 oz.)	½ cup plus 1 tablespoon high grade (4½ oz.) vegetable shortening
1 teaspoon salt	4½ tablespoons iced water

Sift the flour and salt into a mixing bowl. Cut in the shortening with a pastry blender until it looks like a coarse meal. Sprinkle the flour mixture with the iced water and mix slightly. Now gather up half the dough with your hand and form it into a loose ball. Place the ball in the middle of a well floured pastry cloth. Rub flour well onto the rolling pin and roll out the dough into a circle approximately ⅛ inch thick. Do not attempt to turn the crust over and roll it on the other side.

G.K.—7

Slide a spatula under the crust to loosen it from the cloth. Fold it in half, lift it up gently, lay it folded across the center of a 9 inch pie plate, and then unfold it.

For a pre-baked crust, bake for 15 to 20 minutes at 400°. Check once or twice during baking because you want a light golden crust, not a dark brown one.

If the pie is to be filled before baking, place the crust in a hot oven (425°) for 5 minutes or until slightly glazed, then fill and put on the top crust. Make 2 or 3 gashes in it to allow steam to escape, return to a 350° oven and bake until done.

PIE CRUST II

The manufacturers of vegetable shortening have developed a new method of making pie crust which some people think threatens to make the preceding recipe (Pie Crust I) obsolete. This new method uses the same ingredients but the procedure for combining them is different. The great advantages are that it is possible to handle the dough as much as you please, roll it out with ease, and still achieve a tender crust. I am inserting this recipe as an alternate rather than substituting it for the recipe of Pie Crust I because the end product, although excellent, is not the same. It is tender, but it tends to be crumbly rather than flaky. There will be many times when you feel that the particular pie you are making needs one kind of crust rather than the other.

1½ cups sifted all purpose flour	⅓ cup vegetable shortening
½ teaspoon salt	3 tablespoons water

Mix flour and salt in bowl. Cut vegetable shortening into the flour with a fork or pastry blender until the mixture is the consistency of coarse meal. Measure out ¼ cup of this mixture and mix it thoroughly with the water. Now add this paste to the remaining flour-shortening and mix with fork or fingers until dough holds together. Shape into a ball. Place on a lightly floured pastry cloth or board and roll out into the desired size and shape. Bake as directed in preceding recipe.

PUFF PASTE

The method of combining the dough and the butter is the same as that used in making croissants and Danish pastry. The butter must be well washed so that it is plastic and malleable. It must be ice cold and yet soft from having been kneaded and squeezed through your fingers under cold running water or in a bowl of ice water. Do not soften by melting or heating. Do not attempt to make puff paste on a hot summer day. And even on a cold day, chill your working surface by rubbing it with an ice cube.

1 cup sifted flour (4 oz.)	½ teaspoon salt
⅛ to ⅓ cup ice water (2½ oz. plus 1 teaspoon)	½ cup well washed sweet butter (4 oz.)

Put flour on a slab or pastry board that you have chilled. Make a well in the center of the flour, add salt, then pour 2 tablespoons of ice water into the hollow and gradually work in the flour with the fingers and heel of the hand. Continue working in the flour and adding water little by little as needed, about ⅓ cup in all, or the minimum in order to barely hold the dough together. Collect all the dough on the board with a scraper and roll it into a ball. Now lightly flour the scraped-off board. Flatten out the ball of dough with your hand and then roll it out in a rectangle about 10 inches long. In the middle, place the washed butter which has been chilling in the refrigerator while you prepared the dough. Fold one third of the dough over the butter, then fold the remaining third on top of this. Fold in the ends. Roll this rectangle out lengthwise and fold it in thirds again. Turn the dough so that one of the open ends faces front. This is called a turn. Roll out and fold in thirds again, this constitutes two turns. Wrap the dough in waxed paper and chill in the refrigerator for at least 1 hour. You may leave it for several hours or overnight. Repeat this operation two more times, chilling for at least $\frac{1}{2}$ hour in between. After the last chilling roll out the dough into the desired shape. For Napoleons, roll out into a rectangle about $\frac{1}{4}$ inch thick and cut into long strips about 2 inches wide. Place on a baking sheet which has been moistened with water and allow to stand in the refrigerator for $\frac{1}{2}$ hour before baking. Bake in a 400° oven for 15 minutes or until a light golden brown and well puffed.

For patty shells, roll the dough $\frac{1}{4}$ inch thick. Using a 3 inch cutter, cut as many rounds as you want patties. Cut twice as many extra rounds and cut the centers from them with a smaller cutter, making rings. Place two rings on each round, pressing them together gently. Bake the centers of the rings also to use as covers on the shells after they are filled. Place the pastries on a slightly moistened baking sheet. Chill for $\frac{1}{2}$ hour and bake at 400° for 15 minutes or until golden brown and puffy.

GALETTE OR RICH TART PASTRY

In France and Belgium a common dessert is a *Galette* or tart, the European equivalent of our pie. It is a rich flat pastry covered with fruit. In Germany the equivalent is an *obst* (fruit) *küchen*. The pastry is very similar but it is baked in a deeper pan and has more fruit in proportion to the pastry. I will give recipes and directions for making both in the dessert section.

To make the *Galette* pastry:

1 cup sifted all purpose flour (4 oz.)	$\frac{1}{2}$ teaspoon salt
	4 teaspoons sugar

½ cup butter (4 oz.)   2 tablespoons lemon juice
1 egg yolk   2 teaspoons water

Resift the flour into a bowl with the salt and sugar. Work
in the butter with a pastry blender until it is the consistency of a
coarse meal. Beat together with a fork the egg yolk, lemon
juice and water and then blend these into the dry ingredients
with your fingers. Gather the dough together into a ball.
Wrap in wax paper and chill for at least an hour. The dough
may be stored in the refrigerator for several days. When ready
to use, pat out the dough ⅛ inch thick on the bottom and sides
of a shallow (9 by 9 by 1 inch) baking pan, preferably one with
a removable rim. Bake for 10 minutes at 400°. Remove from
oven and cover the dough with the desired fruit and bake as
directed for Blueberry Galette on page (125).

To make *Muerbe Teig:*

1½ cups sifted flour (6 oz.)   ¼ teaspoon salt
2 tablespoons sugar   ½ cup butter (4 oz.)
¼ teaspoon baking powder   1 egg, well beaten

Resift the flour with the sugar, baking powder and salt.
Cut in the butter with a pastry blender or with two knives
until the consistency of a coarse meal. Now work in the well
beaten egg with your fingers. Roll the dough into a ball,
wrap in waxed paper and chill for at least 1 hour. Press
the dough on the bottom and sides of a 9 by 9 by 2 inch
baking pan. Fill with fruit and bake as directed for Peach
Kuchen on page 124.

PÂTE À CHOUX
OR CREAM PUFF PASTE

There is really no trick to making this paste. Once you have
made it, it will become something to turn out when you are

in a hurry or just don't want to fuss or experiment, for it never fails. And please don't limit yourself to using it for cream puffs or éclairs filled with boiled custard or ice cream. Try filling them with a cold *Crème Pâtisserie* (recipe on page 117). And if you do have time to fuss and want to delight and impress family and guests, serve them in a *Croquemboche*, the loveliest of all pastries (recipe on page 120), or try deep fat frying the paste to make *Beignets* (recipe on page 129). The same paste is used to make puffs to fill with creamed fish or meat or with salads of fish or meat. These for either the main course or, if made into tiny puffs, for hors d'oeuvres.

½ cup water (4 oz.)	½ cup sifted all purpose flour
¼ cup butter (2 oz.)	(2 oz.)
⅛ teaspoon salt	2 eggs

Heat the water, add the butter and salt and bring to a rapid boil. Add the sifted flour all at once, lower the heat and beat vigorously with a wooden spoon until the paste comes away from the sides of the pan and forms a smooth ball in the center. *Remove from the heat.* Add the whole egg one at a time, stirring vigorously after each addition until the egg is all absorbed and the batter is thick and glossy. Place large or small spoonfuls of batter, depending on the size puff you want, onto a greased baking sheet 2 inches apart. Bake at 400° for 15 minutes, reduce heat to 300° and continue to bake for 30 minutes longer. Bake miniature puff shells about half the time. Cool before filling. This amount of paste will make 6 large puffs or 12 to 18 smaller puffs.

Just a little helpful note on shaping the puffs—use two spoons, one to scoop up the batter, the other to push the batter off the spoon onto the baking sheet. When making éclairs, place one teaspoonful of batter slightly overlapping the other at one end, then with a spatula smooth over the sides and top into the long éclair shape.

Desserts

PROBABLY no cook ever has enough dessert recipes to keep herself and her family interested in the end of the meal and happy when it is over. It has been my experience that more women are interested in learning new ways to prepare desserts than any other type of food. A special volume could be written on desserts alone. But this seems unnecessary for, once again, it seems to me the most useful role for a cookbook is not to be an encyclopedia but rather to be a careful selection of a manageable group of varied and exciting dishes so chosen as to provide the imaginative cook with a basic and trustworthy selection and a point of departure for creating new recipes of her own.

This section, therefore, is limited to some 50 recipes. Some are what seem to me better ways for making standard items. Others are for the uncommon things—foods you may have seen in pictures or eaten in better restaurants, but probably never dreamed of making in your own home. Perhaps the recipes were not readily available or, if available, were frighteningly complex. Browse first in these pages to see how simple the seemingly complex dessert recipe can be. Then toss away your fears and start using them. Many recipes which you might expect to find here, such as crêpes suzettes, babas, upside down cakes, tortes, are omitted because they can be found in my earlier book, *Meals for Guests*.

It seems wise to start with a sponge cake. A very ordinary thing, sponge cake, but when properly prepared, a delectable thing too. Moreover, around a good sponge cake literally scores of other desserts can be built. A few of these variations will be given below and you should be able to add distinguished items of your own. You will find that this particular cake keeps in superb condition in your home freezer, and it can be so quickly thawed and "dressed up" that you will find it a most convenient way to meet the unexpected guest problem.

SPONGE CAKE

6 eggs	1 cup sifted cake flour (3¾ oz.)
1 cup sugar (8 oz.)	1 teaspoon baking powder
1 tablespoon lemon juice	¼ teaspoon salt

Have the eggs at room temperature. Separate the egg whites from the egg yolks, placing the whites in a large mixing bowl. Whip the whites until they stand in stiff peaks and are glossy. Gradually beat ½ cup of sugar into the stiff whites. Add the lemon juice to the yolks in another bowl and beat until thick and lemon colored. Beat the remaining ½ cup of sugar into the yolks. Fold the egg yolk mixture gently into the whites. Sift flour, salt and baking powder together 4 times. Now gently fold the flour mixture, ¼ cup at a time, into the eggs. Pour into a 9 inch ungreased angel food pan, or into two ungreased 8 by 4 inch bread pans. Bake one hour at 325°. Cool in the pan.

SPONGE CAKE WITH FRUIT AND WHIPPED CREAM

A simple and always welcome dessert is sponge cake covered with fresh or frozen fruit and topped with sweetened whipped cream. Partially defrosted frozen peaches are particularly good. If you wish to add a note of glamour, pour a little cointreau or kirsch over the fruit.

BAVARIAN CREAM

A lovely cool concoction to serve plain or decorated with berries or fruit. This ever welcome treat can be produced in various flavors and lovely colors. The equally familiar dessert, Charlotte Russe, is just Bavarian Cream adorned with small sticks or slices of sponge cake or with lady fingers. To make a heavier, richer cream omit the egg whites, as the French usually do.

VANILLA BAVARIAN CREAM

1 envelope or 1 tablespoon gelatin	1 cup milk
¼ cup cold water	1 teaspoon vanilla
4 egg yolks	2 egg whites
½ cup sugar	1 cup heavy cream

Soften 1 envelope gelatin in the cold water. Beat the egg yolks and sugar together with a wooden spoon until they are thick and creamy. Heat the milk to the boiling point, then add it very gradually to the egg yolk mixture. Stirring constantly cook this custard over low heat or in a double boiler, stirring constantly, until it is thick and smooth. Add the vanilla and the softened gelatin and stir until the gelatin is dissolved. Cool the mixture. Beat the egg whites until stiff. Whip the cream. Fold the stiffly beaten egg whites and the whipped cream into the cooled custard. Pour into a 9 inch ring mold rinsed with cold water. Chill in the refrigerator for at least 3 hours. When ready to serve, unmold on a serving platter and garnish with fresh or frozen fruit. Whole strawberries or raspberries make an especially pretty garnish.

CHOCOLATE BAVARIAN CREAM

Follow the directions for vanilla Bavarian Cream. When you add the gelatin also add 6 ounces semi-sweet chocolate melted with 1 tablespoon cream over hot water. This can be molded as it is, but is especially good if you line the mold with fingers of angel food cake, thus making a Charlotte Russe. Unmold and garnish with shaved sweet chocolate and dabs of whipped cream.

COFFEE BAVARIAN CREAM

Follow the directions for vanilla Bavarian Cream, but omit the vanilla and add $2\frac{1}{2}$ tablespoons of instant coffee powder at the same time you add the softened gelatin.

FRUIT BAVARIAN CREAM

2 cups puréed fruit	1 envelope gelatin
$\frac{1}{2}$ cup sugar	$\frac{1}{4}$ cup water
1 tablespoon lemon juice or kirsch	1 cup heavy cream
	Whole berries or sliced fruit

Thoroughly mash fresh or frozen fruit, either strawberries, raspberries or peaches, to make 2 cups of fruit purée. Add lemon juice or kirsch and sugar to taste—usually $\frac{1}{2}$ cup of sugar is sufficient. Soften gelatin in cold water and then place over hot water until the gelatin is completely dissolved. Add the gelatin to the fruit mixture. Mix well. Whip the cream. When the mixture begins to set, fold in the whipped cream. Pour into a mold rinsed in cold water. Allow to chill in the refrigerator for at least 3 hours. Unmold on a serving dish and garnish with whole berries or slices of peaches.

CHARLOTTE RUSSE

A dressed up Bavarian Cream. Line a mold with finger shaped slices of sponge cake or with lady fingers. Fill it half full of the Bavarian Cream of your choice, cover with a layer of sponge cake or lady fingers. Fill to the top with Bavarian Cream and put into the refrigerator to chill for at least 3 hours. It may be made as much as a day in advance. For an airier, less rich filling, fold 4 beaten egg whites, instead of 2, into the cream.

MACAROON CREAM

1 envelope or 1 tablespoon
gelatin
½ cup cold milk
1½ cups hot milk
½ teaspoon salt
2 egg yolks

¼ teaspoon almond extract
4 tablespoons sugar
1 cup almond macaroon crumbs
2 egg whites, stiffly beaten
Whipped cream garnish

Soften gelatin in the cold milk. Add the very hot milk and salt. Place in a heavy pan over low heat or in the top of a double boiler over boiling water and stir until the softened gelatin is thoroughly dissolved. Beat the egg yolks and slowly stir a little of the hot milk mixture into them. When the yolks are warmed sufficiently to keep them from curdling, add them slowly to the hot milk mixture, stirring constantly. Cook, stirring constantly, until the mixture coats the spoon. Remove from heat. Add almond extract and sugar. Stir until sugar is dissolved. Stir in 1 cup of almond macaroon crumbs. Chill until almost set. Then fold in the stiffly beaten egg whites. Pour in a mold rinsed in cold water. Allow to chill until firm in the refrigerator for at least 3 hours. Unmold onto a serving platter. Garnish with dabs of whipped cream and, for added glamor, whole fresh strawberries.

CHOCOLATE MACAROON CREAM

A wonderful combination of flavors. Follow directions for Macaroon Cream, adding 6 ounces of semi-sweet chocolate, melted, along with the softened gelatin. Use only $\frac{1}{2}$ cup of macaroon crumbs and line the mold with whole macaroons. Unmold and garnish with whipped cream and grated sweet chocolate. To give a further gourmet touch, flavor the whipped cream with crème de cacao.

LEMON CHIFFON PIE

Chiffon pies make delicious desserts, particularly in hot weather or after a rich heavy meal. There are as many chiffon fillings as there are flavors. These are my two favorites.

A baked 9 inch pie shell (page 97)	$\frac{1}{2}$ teaspoon salt
1 envelope or 1 tablespoon gelatin	1 tablespoon grated lemon rind (optional)
$\frac{1}{4}$ cup cold water	1 cup heavy cream
5 large eggs, separated	2 tablespoons sugar
1 cup sugar	$\frac{1}{4}$ teaspoon vanilla
$\frac{2}{3}$ cup lemon juice	

Soften gelatin in water. In a heavy pan beat the egg yolks, $\frac{1}{2}$ cup sugar, lemon juice and salt. Cook over low heat, stirring constantly, until mixture is thickened to the consistency of a boiled custard. Remove from heat, add the softened gelatin and stir until it is dissolved. Add the grated rind. Cool the mixture in the refrigerator until it just begins to jell. Make a meringue by beating the egg whites until stiff and then gradually beating in $\frac{1}{2}$ cup sugar. Fold the meringue into the jelled mixture. Pile lightly into a baked pie shell. Whip the heavy cream, flavor with the sugar and vanilla. Spread top of pie with whipped cream.

LIME CHIFFON PIE

Follow directions for Lemon Chiffon Pie, substituting ⅔ cup lime juice for the lemon juice and adding 3 or 4 drops of green food coloring.

BLACK AND WHITE CHIFFON PIE

A fabulous dessert whose appearance at the end of a meal always commands a moment of silence. Alternate layers of chocolate chiffon and rum cream piled in a baked pie shell at a height of at least 4 inches, topped with whipped cream and shaved sweet chocolate.

A baked 9 inch pie shell
Chocolate chiffon filling
Rum cream filling

Whipped cream, sweetened
Shaved sweet chocolate

CHOCOLATE CHIFFON

2 envelopes gelatin
3 cups milk
⅜ cup sugar
¼ teaspoon salt

9 ounces bittersweet chocolate
2 tablespoons light cream
4 egg whites, stiffly beaten

Soften gelatin in ½ cup cold milk. Heat 2½ cups milk with the sugar and salt. Add the softened gelatin to the hot milk and stir until dissolved. Cool this mixture. While it is cooling, melt the bittersweet chocolate with the cream in the top of a double boiler, then stir it into the gelatin mixture. Chill in refrigerator. When the mixture has just begun to jell, beat it until frothy and then fold in the stiffly beaten egg whites.

RUM CREAM

1 envelope or 1 tablespoon gelatin	⅞ cup sugar
½ cup cold water	½ cup rum
5 egg yolks	2 egg whites, stiffly beaten
	1 cup heavy cream, whipped

Soften gelatin in cold water. Beat the egg yolks until light, gradually stir in the sugar and beat until thick and creamy. Bring the gelatin and water mixture to a boil and then, stirring constantly, add it slowly to the egg yolk mixture. Stir in the rum, fold in stiffly beaten egg whites and whipped cream.

Allow both fillings to chill until almost completely set and then, starting with one-half the chocolate chiffon, pile them in alternate layers into a baked 9 inch pie shell prepared according to directions on page 97. Chill the pie in the refrigerator for at least 2 hours—it may be allowed to stand overnight. When ready to serve, spread the top with whipped cream sweetened to taste and flavored with vanilla, and sprinkle the top with grated or shaved sweet chocolate.

ORANGE WHIP

A cool airy dessert, perfect after a heavy meal and unbelievably simple to prepare.

3 egg yolks	1 envelope or 1 tablespoon gelatin
¾ cup sugar	3 egg whites, stiffly beaten
¾ cup orange juice	2 cups heavy cream, whipped
1 teaspoon grated orange rind	

Beat egg yolks well, gradually add the sugar continuing to beat until the mixture is thick and creamy. Add ½ cup orange juice and beat well. Soften gelatin in ¼ cup orange juice and then melt it over hot water. Add the melted gelatin to the egg yolk mixture, stirring well. Fold in egg whites beaten until stiff and glossy and heavy cream beaten until it stands in soft peaks. This whip is too light to unmold so pour it directly into the deep serving bowl and allow it to chill in the refrigerator for at least 2 hours. It may be made as long as a day in advance.

ORANGE FLOAT

An easy unpretentious dessert. A great comfort to have in your repertoire for those occasions when you aren't feeling particularly creative but still want to end your meal with a light touch.

3 navel oranges	3 tablespoons flour
1 cup orange juice	1½ tablespoons cornstarch
⅛ cup sugar	3 egg yolks
1½ cups milk	1 tablespoon butter
¾ cup sugar	1 teaspoon vanilla

Peel the oranges, removing all excess membrane. Slice the oranges into thin slices and arrange them in a large serving bowl. Sprinkle the slices with sugar and pour the orange juice over them.

Heat the milk to the boiling point. Mix together the sugar, flour and cornstarch. Gradually stir the hot milk into this dry mixture. Return to the heat and cook, stirring constantly, until the mixture thickens. Beat the egg yolks slightly and stir them carefully into the hot mixture. Continue to stir and cook for 1 minute. Stir in the butter. Cool the pudding, stir in the vanilla and pour it over the oranges in the serving dish. It will float in the juice. Chill well before serving. Sweetened whipped cream makes delicious topping for the float but it is not essential to its goodness.

LEMON FROMAGE

A cool, tart dessert that is a pleasure to make as well as to eat. Fromage means cheese, but the term here refers to consistency rather than content.

3 eggs
2 egg yolks
½ cup sugar
Grated rind of lemon

¾ tablespoon gelatin
Juice of 2 lemons
2 cups heavy cream
Berries

Place whole eggs and egg yolks in a bowl and beat vigorously until light and frothy. While beating, gradually add the cup sugar and continue to beat until mixture is thick and pale. Add the grated lemon rind. Soften gelatin in the lemon juice, then melt it over hot water. When thoroughly melted, add the gelatin and lemon juice to the egg mixture and beat well. Fold in cream whipped until very stiff. Pour into a quart size mold, preferably a melon shaped one, and chill until firm in the refrigerator for at least 4 hours. Unmold onto a serving platter and garnish with whole berries, strawberries, raspberries or blueberries.

COFFEE PUDDING

This dessert deserves a much fancier name, at least an "à la something or other", but it is so very simple to make that I am afraid a fancy name might mislead you enough to keep you from trying it. That is too great a risk to take; so simple coffee pudding it will remain.

24 marshmallows
¾ cup very strong coffee
¾ pint heavy cream

3 tablespoons crème de cacao
Shaved or grated semi-sweet
    chocolate

Put the marshmallows and coffee in the top of a double boiler and heat over boiling water until the marshmallows are completely melted. Stir well and cool to room temperature. Whip the cream until stiff and fold it into the cooled mixture. Stir in the crème de cacao. Pour into a large serving bowl or into 6 sherbet glasses. Garnish the top with the shaved or grated chocolate. Chill for at least 4 hours before serving.

CHOCOLATE MARSHMALLOW CAKE

20 marshmallows
½ cup milk
2 ounces bitter chocolate, grated coarsely

¾ cup pecans, chopped coarsely
1 cup heavy cream, whipped
Sponge cake or lady fingers
Shaved sweet chocolate

Place marshmallows and milk in the top of a double boiler and melt over boiling water. Cool. Fold in coarsely grated bitter chocolate and chopped pecans. Fold in cream, whipped until stiff. Line a mold with strips of sponge cake or lady fingers. Fill with the marshmallow mixture and allow to chill for at least 6 hours. It may be made as far as a day in advance. Unmold onto a serving platter and garnish with shaved or grated sweet chocolate.

APRICOT PACK

An ice cream dessert with a difference, very easy to prepare and impressive to serve.

1 eleven ounce package of dried apricots

Sugar to taste
1½ pints vanilla ice cream

Cook the dried apricots according to directions on the package. When they are soft, sugar them to taste—different brands require varying amounts of sugar. Mash them well or force

G.K.—8

through a sieve or strainer. Cool. When cool, spread the purée of apricots in the bottom of a standard sized refrigerator tray. Cover with vanilla ice cream—usually requires 1 to 1½ pints, and freeze the two together. When ready to serve, unmold onto a serving platter. This is equally good made with straw-berries or raspberries if you add one tablespoon of dissolved gelatin per 2 cups of puréed sweetened fruit.

RUM SOUR CREAM MOUSSE

A gourmet dessert that you mix in a minute and rave about for hours.

1 pint commercial sour cream	6 tablespoons melted sweet
1 tablespoon rum	chocolate
½ cup coarsely crumbled almond	½ cup sugar
macaroons	1 teaspoon vanilla
	Shaved sweet chocolate

Mix all these ingredients together thoroughly, turn into a refrigerator tray and freeze until solid—this usually takes at least 3 hours. It may be made several days in advance. When ready to serve, unmold onto a serving platter and garnish with shaved sweet chocolate.

HOT BUTTERSCOTCH SUNDAE

Ice cream is a great institution and topped with a creamy rich butterscotch it becomes even greater.

1 beaten egg yolk	⅔ cup brown sugar
¼ cup butter	¼ cup light corn syrup
¼ cup water	

Combine all the ingredients in the top of a double boiler. Mix well and cook over boiling water until thick, stirring frequently. This sauce may be made in advance and reheated before serving or it can be served cold.

CHARTREUSE CUSTARD

A light exotic dessert—and even if you don't like chartreuse as a liqueur, you will give hearty assent to this use of it.

1 cup milk	6 egg yolks
2 tablespoons sugar	2 tablespoons heavy cream
3 tablespoons chartreuse— preferably yellow chartreuse	

Mix the milk, sugar and chartreuse together in the top of a double boiler. Keep the water in the bottom of the boiler simmering. While this milk mixture is heating, beat the egg yolks and cream together until light and creamy. Pour the hot milk very gradually into the beaten egg yolks, stirring constantly. Return the mixture to the top of the double boiler and cook, continuing to stir, until mixture just coats the spoon. Line 6 sherbet glasses with strips of sponge cake or with lady fingers and fill with the custard. Serve either warm or chilled.

CRÈME BRÛLÉE

A popular French dessert that is so good and so easy to make that it should have gained wide acclaim in this country long before now.

3 cups heavy cream	6 egg yolks
1 teaspoon vanilla	1 cup sugar

Heat the cream and vanilla in a heavy pan over very low heat. Beat the egg yolks and 6 tablespoons sugar together until very creamy and light. Add the warm cream very slowly and carefully to the egg yolks, stirring constantly. Return to a heavy pan and continue to cook and stir over low heat until the mixture coats the back of a spoon as it is lifted straight upwards. Do not cook past this point or the custard will curdle. Pour the custard into a shallow glass baking dish, 2 by 6 by 8 inches. Put into the refrigerator to chill overnight. Next day cover the top completely with the remainder of the sugar. Be sure none of the custard shows through. Place it under a hot broiler until the sugar is caramelized. Watch it carefully during this process or the sugar will burn. It may be served immediately or it may be chilled again before serving.

MALAKOFF

A caramelized egg white mold floating atop a smooth soft custard. A dessert that is truly as light as air and as good as it is unusual.

2 tablespoons water	6 egg yolks
1 cup sugar	$\frac{1}{2}$ cup sugar
6 egg whites	1 teaspoon vanilla
3 cups milk	

First make the caramel mold. Put 2 tablespoons water and 1 cup sugar into a heavy pan, place it on very low heat and cook, without stirring, until it turns a golden caramel color. While the sugar is caramelizing, beat the egg whites until very stiff. When the sugar has turned a golden caramel color, take it off the heat and immediately start dripping it into the stiff whites, continuing to beat at high speed. When all the caramel has been beaten into the egg whites, pour this golden meringue into a well buttered 8 inch ring mold. Chill for at least 2 hours before serving.

Now make your custard sauce. Heat the milk and vanilla in a heavy pan. Combine the egg yolks and sugar and beat slightly. Pour the hot milk very slowly and carefully into the egg yolk mixture, stirring constantly. Return the mixture to the heavy pan and cook over low heat until the mixture just coats the spoon. Be careful not to cook beyond this point or the custard will curdle. Set in the refrigerator to chill.

To serve the Malakoff, unmold the meringue onto a rather deep serving plate or platter. Pour the custard very slowly around it. As soon as the meringue, which is very light, begins to float, you have enough custard. Serve the remaining custard in a separate bowl.

NAPOLEONS

Don't restrict your enjoyment of these flaky delicacies to an occasional meal in a French restaurant. Your own Napoleons will be even better. Follow directions on page 99 for making puff paste. Roll and bake as directed there for Napoleons. Cut each baked strip into pieces 3 inches long. Now take each piece and split it into 3 or 4 layers. Spread each layer, except the top one, with crème pâtisserie and push them lightly together. Sprinkle the top of each Napoleon with confectioners' sugar.

CRÈME PÂTISSERIE

1 egg	½ cup sugar
1 egg yolk	1 teaspoon vanilla
1 tablespoon flour	1 cup hot milk
1 envelope or 1 tablespoon gelatin	2 egg whites, stiffly beaten
	1 cup heavy cream, whipped

Put the egg, egg yolk, flour and sugar into a bowl and beat them well together. Then mix in the dry gelatin and vanilla. Pour the hot milk very slowly into the egg mixture, stirring constantly. Cook over low heat, continuing to stir until mixture just comes to the boiling point. Remove from the heat and cool. Chill until it begins to thicken, then add the stiffly beaten egg whites and whipped cream.

SOUFFLÉ AU COINTREAU
(OR GRAND MARNIER)

Do not feel that a soufflé is a dessert that has to wait for a daring moment. There is only one trick to a successful soufflé and that is to be able to eat it the minute it is removed from the oven. A soufflé waits for no one.

2 tablespoons butter
1 tablespoon flour
½ cup hot milk (4 oz.)
½ teaspoon vanilla
5 egg yolks
⅓ cup sugar (2½ oz. + 1 teaspoon)

6 egg whites, stiffly beaten
2 tablespoons sugar
Strips of sponge cake or lady fingers (optional)
½ cup cointreau or grand marnier

Melt the butter in a sauce pan, slowly stir in the flour and cook for 1 minute. Gradually stir in the hot milk and vanilla and stir over low heat for 4 minutes until thick and smooth. Beat the egg yolk together with ⅓ cup sugar. Slowly and carefully stir in the hot sauce. Set aside while you beat the egg whites until very stiff. After they are stiff, gradually beat in 2 table-spoons of sugar. Now fold the egg whites lightly into the egg yolk mixture until they are completely incorporated. Butter a quart soufflé mold or a straight sided glass baking dish— sprinkle bottom and sides with granulated sugar. Pour in half of the soufflé mixture. Cover with strips of sponge cake or lady fingers soaked in the cointreau. Pour the remaining liqueur over the cake. Fill the mold with remaining soufflé mixture. The dish should be level full so that while baking it will rise high above the rim. Bake at 400° for 25 to 35 minutes, depending on how well-done you like your soufflé. Serve immediately upon taking from the oven. It is extra good if accompanied with a bowl of custard sauce flavored with the liqueur you used in the soufflé. Make the boiled custard according to the directions on page 117, cutting the recipe in half. If you wish to omit the cake, stir the cointreau directly into the egg mixture.

If you have slightly more soufflé than your dish will hold, wrap a 3 inch wide strip of well-buttered aluminium foil around the top, giving your dish extra depth. The strip peels off easily leaving you with a high soufflé.

CHOCOLATE SOUFFLÉ

2 tablespoons flour	¼ cup sugar
1½ tablespoons butter	1 teaspoon vanilla
¾ cup milk, scalded (6 oz.)	5 egg yolks, beaten
1½ ounces chocolate, melted	5 egg whites, stiffly beaten

Melt the butter, stir in the flour slowly until you have a smooth roux. Gradually blend in the scalded milk mixed with the sugar, melted chocolate and vanilla. (If you like a stronger chocolate flavor, use 2 ounces of chocolate. If less strong, use 1 ounce.) Stir over low heat until the mixture thickens. Remove from the heat. Carefully stir a little of the hot mixture into the beaten egg yolks to warm them. Stirring constantly, add the egg yolk mixture gradually to the hot milk mixture. Allow to cool for a few minutes and then fold in the stiffly beaten egg whites. Put the mixture into a soufflé mold buttered and dusted generously with sugar. Bake at 350° for 25 to 30 minutes. It must be served immediately upon being taken from the oven, so time it correctly. Again the caution, a soufflé waits for no one.

COFFEE SOUFFLÉ

Prepare as for chocolate soufflé, substituting 3 tablespoons powdered coffee for the chocolate.

CROQUEMBOCHE

A thrill to make, to look at and, most important, to eat.

Follow directions on page 101 for making *Pâté à Choux* or cream puff paste. Make the cream puffs about the size of walnuts. Cool the puffs and fill them with a vanilla Bavarian Cream, page 105. Make a caramel syrup according to directions below. Once the syrup is caramel colored, you must work fast because it hardens rather quickly. Dip the bottoms of the puffs, one at a time, into the hot caramel syrup and arrange a row around the edge of a serving plate dusted with confectioners' sugar. Place a second row of puffs over the spaces between the first row of puffs. The same with the third row, etc., until you have built a pyramid topped with a single puff. Drip the remaining caramel syrup over the pyramid and sprinkle the whole liberally with confectioners' sugar.

CARAMEL SYRUP

1 cup sugar   ¼ teaspoon cream of tartar
¼ cup water

Combine the ingredients in a heavy bottomed sauce pan and cook over low heat, without stirring, until the syrup turns amber. Keep the syrup hot over boiling water while working with it.

CHERRIES JUBILEE ON ICE CREAM

Pour the juice from a No. 1 can of pitted black bing cherries into a pan or the top of a chafing dish. Bring the juice to a boil and thicken it with cornstarch dissolved in a little cold water—it usually takes 1 teaspoon of cornstarch. Add the cherries to the thickened juice and stir until they are heated through. Pour $\frac{1}{3}$ cup of kirsch over the cherries and blaze. Scoop vanilla ice cream into sherbet glasses, mask with the cherries and sauce. If you have a chafing dish it is nice to blaze the cherries and serve them up at the table.

APPLE PIE

The most popular pie in America, and with good reason, if and when it is a good apple pie. Taking for granted a tender, flaky crust, a requisite for any pie, the success of an apple pie depends on the quality of the apple. There is a long period each year when it is well not to bake apple pies—that is from January, when the last of the firm Winesaps are gone, until June when the Transparent Greens come into the market. The early Green apples make a delicious tart pie, but it is of a different consistency from the later, firmer apples. The slices tend to cook down to a mush. Wealthies, which are the next good pie apple, tend to do the same thing. Both of these apples require a bit more flour than the later, firmer apples. Jonathans and Winesaps, which follow, are the best of the later pie apples. Winesaps are usually available until after Christmas, becoming more expensive of course as the season advances. The slices in these apples retain their shape during baking, giving the pie a different look and texture from the earlier apples. They are good, however. MacIntosh apples which are available for a long period have the consistency of early Green apples without their tart flavor. They need a tablespoon or 2 of lemon juice to make an acceptable pie. Rome Beauties and Red Romes are best avoided.

To make one 9 inch pie, prepare pastry for a double crust pie according to directions on page 98.

Line the pie plate with pastry, sprinkle with sugar and bake for 10 minutes at 400°, long enough to give the crust a glaze. Then fill with peeled, cored and sliced apples. To make a good full bodied pie, fill it heaping full. It will most likely boil over a bit, but if you place a large sheet of aluminium foil underneath the pie, there will be no cleaning up problem.

The amount of flour and sugar used depend on the tartness and juiciness of the apple. The early apples require more of both —usually 1 cup of sugar and 3 tablespoons of flour sprinkled over the apples. (For Jonathan and Winesaps, use $\frac{1}{2}$ to $\frac{2}{3}$ cup sugar and 2 tablespoons flour.) Then sprinkle with $\frac{1}{2}$ to 1 teaspoonful cinnamon, according to taste, and dot with butter. Cover the pie with the top crust, cut 3 or 4 gashes in the crust to allow steam to escape. Bake at 350° for $\frac{3}{4}$ to 1 hour. If you are using apples that are not tart or flavorful, sprinkle them with lemon juice.

Apple pie is best served warm. It may be baked in advance and reheated just before serving. It will keep in a freezer for months.

SOUR CREAM PIE

A stand-by in our grandmothers' day but much neglected of late, which is too bad because it is a delicious dessert in spite of its homely quality.

Prepare pastry for one 9 inch pie according to directions on page 98. Line the pie plate with pastry, sprinkle it with sugar and bake at 400° for 10 minutes or until it has a slight glaze. This will prevent the crust from getting soggy. Prepare the following mixture:

3 eggs	½ cup raisins
1 cup sugar	1 tablespoon lemon juice
2 cups commercial sour cream	¼ teaspoon salt

Beat the eggs well, add the sugar and the other ingredients, stir well together and pour into the pie crust. Bake at 325° for 50 minutes. Serve cold.

RHUBARB CUSTARD PIE

Another old-timer that too few of the younger generation know about.

Prepare pastry for a 2 crust pie according to directions on page 98. Line a 9 inch pie plate with pastry, sprinkle with sugar and bake at 400° for 10 minutes or until slightly glazed.

4 cups young unpeeled rhubarb cut into ½ inch pieces	1½ cups sugar
2 tablespoons flour	3 beaten eggs

Put the rhubarb into the pie shell. Mix together the other ingredients and pour over the rhubarb. Cover with the top crust. Make several gashes in the crust to permit escape of steam. Bake at 350° for 45 minutes or until custard is set.

CREAM CHEESE PEACH TARTS

Prepare pastry according to directions on page 98. Line six 3 inch tart shells with pastry and bake at 375° for 15 minutes or until done.

5 ounces cream cheese
3 tablespoons sugar
1 teaspoon lemon juice
½ cup heavy cream, whipped stiff

½ cup currant jelly
¼ cup raspberry jelly
3 large peaches, peeled and halved

Soften the cream cheese at room temperature. Gradually beat in the sugar and beat until fluffy. Stir in the lemon juice. Fold in the whipped cream. Now divide this mixture among the tart shells. Chill in the refrigerator for 1 hour. Combine the currant jelly and the raspberry jelly in a large bottomed pan and melt over low heat. Add the peach halves and simmer slowly for 5 minutes. Place a peach half, cut side down, on top of the cream cheese mixture in each tart shell. Cool the jelly a little and then spoon it over the peaches to give them a rosy glaze. Chill well.

PEACH KUCHEN

Prepare *Muerbe Teig* pastry according to directions on page 101. Press the pastry on the bottom and sides of a greased 2 to 3 inch deep pan, 9 inches square.

12 peach halves (canned or fresh)
¾ cup light brown sugar
1 teaspoon cinnamon

2 egg yolks
1 cup heavy cream
Whipped cream garnish

Place the 12 peach halves on the dough, cut side up and sprinkle with the combined brown sugar and cinnamon. Bake at 400° for 15 minutes. Now mix together the egg yolks, slightly beaten, and the heavy cream. Pour this over the peaches and continue to bake for 30 minutes at 350°. Cool. Serve with whipped cream.

BLUEBERRY TART

Prepare *Galette* dough according to the directions on page 100. Cover the bottom of a 9 inch pie plate with the pastry, and after chilling it bake at 400° for 10 minutes. Then cover with a mixture of:

3 cups blueberries	1 tablespoon flour
½ cup sugar	2 tablespoons lemon juice

Return to a 350° oven and bake for another 20 minutes. It is good as it is or served cold with a topping of whipped cream. However, it is even more delicious if covered with a thick custard, as follows:

½ cup light cream	2 tablespoons sugar
2 egg yolks, slightly beaten	½ teaspoon salt

Mix all the ingredients together in a sauce pan and cook over low heat, stirring constantly until thickened. Cool the custard and pour it over the slightly cooled tart. Whipped cream on top of the custard may seem like gilding the lily, but there is nothing wrong with a gilded lily.

Sour cherries may be substituted for the blueberries, in which case increase the amount of sugar to 1 cup and use ¼ teaspoon almond extract instead of the lemon juice.

CREAM TART

A combination of cake and meringue baked at the same time produces a thoroughly beautiful and delicious dessert, especially if put together with a fruit or sour cream filling.

1½ cups sugar (12 oz.)
¼ cup butter (2 oz.)
4 egg yolks
½ teaspoon vanilla
1 cup sifted cake flour (3¾ oz.)
2 teaspoons baking powder
¼ teaspoon salt

5 tablespoons light cream
4 egg whites
⅛ teaspoon salt
1 teaspoon vanilla
½ cup almonds, blanched and
    coarsely shredded (2 oz.)

Cream the butter and ½ cup of sugar together. Beat in the egg yolks one at a time. Add ½ teaspoon vanilla. Sift the flour, baking powder and salt together. Add the dry ingredients to the egg yolk mixture alternately with the cream. Beat the batter until very smooth. Spread it evenly in 2 greased 9 inch layer cake pans. Now make a meringue by beating the egg whites and salt until they are stiff and stand in soft glossy peaks and then beating in very slowly the remaining cup of sugar, 1 tablespoon at a time, and 1 teaspoon vanilla. Spread the meringue evenly over the cake batter in both pans. Stud the top of one of the meringues with the ½ cup of almonds that you have blanched and shredded coarsely. Bake at 325° for 25 minutes, then increase the heat to 350° and bake for another 25 minutes. Cool the cake in the pan. When ready to serve, place one layer on a serving plate, cover with an apricot or sour cream filling. Place the almond studded layer on top of the filling and, if using a fruit filling, garnish with whipped cream. If using the sour cream filling, reserve some of the filling for a garnish.

APRICOT FILLING

Cook 1½ cups dried apricots until soft, add sugar to taste and mash to a fine purée. Cool the apricot purée and then fold in ½ cup heavy cream whipped until stiff.

SOUR CREAM FILLING

1 egg yolk
3 tablespoons sugar
1 tablespoon cornstarch

1 cup sour cream
½ teaspoon vanilla

Beat the egg yolk slightly. Add the sugar and cornstarch. Mix. Stir in the sour cream and cook over low heat until it coats the spoon. Flavor with the ½ teaspoon vanilla. Cool before spreading on the tart.

RUM NUT TORTE

1 cup sugar (8 oz.)
5 egg yolks
½ cup blanched and chopped almonds (2 oz.)
½ teaspoon baking powder
2 cups fine zwieback crumbs (8 oz.)

½ teaspoon vanilla
1 tablespoon lemon juice
¼ cup rum (2 oz.)
5 egg whites
Rum syrup (recipe given below)
1 cup heavy cream, whipped
2 tablespoons sugar

Beat together the sugar and egg yolks. Stir in the almonds, zwieback crumbs, baking powder, vanilla, lemon juice and rum. Beat the egg whites until stiff and fold them lightly into the batter. Pour the batter into a well greased 6 or 7 inch spring form pan. Bake for 1 hour at 300°. Allow the cake to cool and then split it into 3 layers. Sprinkle each layer with 2 tablespoons of rum syrup and put the layers together with sweetened whipped cream. Reserve enough of the whipped cream to garnish the top.

RUM SYRUP

To make a rum syrup, cook together for 10 minutes ¼ cup (2 oz.) water and ½ cup (4 oz.) sugar. Cool and flavor with ¼ cup (2 oz.) rum.

CHEESE CAKE

There are literally dozens of different recipes for cheese cake, but they usually fall into one of two categories: the moist, rich and not so high type, and the light, spongy, high cheese cake. I am giving my best recipe for each type. The crusts for cheese cake vary too; from a regular kuchen, pastry crust or graham cracker crust to a light crumb lining in the pan. I prefer the latter, and unless you have a preference, just butter your cake pan heavily and then sprinkle it generously with fine zwieback crumbs, fill and bake as directed.

MOIST CHEESE CAKE

8 ounces cottage cheese	½ teaspoon vanilla
8 ounces cream cheese	1½ cups sour cream
⅔ cup sugar	4 tablespoons sugar
4 whole eggs	½ teaspoon vanilla

Have the cheese at room temperature. Mash or beat the cottage cheese until it is fine and smooth. Now mix together the cream cheese and cottage cheese, ⅔ cup of sugar, eggs and ½ teaspoon of vanilla. Pour the mixture into a crumb lined 9 inch cake pan and bake at 375° for 25 minutes. Remove from the oven allow to stand for 5 minutes. Cover with a mixture of the sour cream, remaining sugar and vanilla. Return to oven and bake at 450° for 5 minutes. Serve cold.

AIRY CHEESE CAKE

16 ounces cream cheese or 8 oz. cream cheese and 8 oz. cottage cheese	2 tablespoons flour
	1¼ cups sugar (10 oz.)
	1 teaspoon vanilla
1⅔ cups sour cream	5 egg whites, stiffly beaten
5 egg yolks, beaten	

Have the cream cheese at room temperature. Mix the cream cheese, sour cream, beaten egg yolks, flour, sugar and vanilla together until smooth and creamy. Fold in the stiffly beaten egg whites. Pour into a deep (at least 3 inches) 9 inch crumb lined cake pan, preferably a spring form. Bake at 325° for ½ hour, lower heat to 300° and bake another ½ hour. Turn off heat and allow cake to cool in the oven. (Remove rim of spring form.) Serve cold.

MOCK CHEESE CAKE

Not to be scorned because it isn't the real thing. By any other name it would taste as good.

4 eggs, separated	Zweiback (or graham cracker
1 No. 2 can applesauce	crumbs)
1 14 ounce can condensed milk	2 tablespoons sugar
4 tablespoons lemon juice	1 tablespoon cinnamon

Beat the egg yolks well. Add the applesauce, condensed milk and lemon juice and mix together thoroughly. Whip the egg whites until stiff and glossy and fold them into the mixture. Pour the batter into a 9 by 9 by 2 inch cake pan buttered and lined with zwieback or graham cracker crumbs. Sprinkle the top with a mixture of 2 tablespoons crumbs and the cinnamon and sugar. Bake at 350° for 1 hour. Allow the cake to cool at room temperature. Chill before serving.

BEIGNETS

Prepare a Pâte à Choux dough according to directions on page 101. Flavor the dough with 1 teaspoon vanilla or with 1 tablespoon rum or brandy.

G.K.—9

Drop the dough by the rounded teaspoonful into hot deep fat (370°). Fry the Beignets for about 4 minutes or until they are golden. Drain on absorbent paper. Serve immediately, sprinkled with confectioners' sugar or with a custard or fruit sauce.

MERINGUES

Meringues fall into two categories. Crisp Meringues that are baked as tart shells (large or small) or as "Kisses" (small pointed meringues), and Soft Meringues that are baked as toppings for pies and other desserts. Both these easy, delicious desserts too often are unnecessary failures. The Crisp Meringues may crack or be sticky, the Soft Meringues "weep" or fall. The success of any meringue depends on proper beating, the correct baking temperature and baking time. Beat the egg whites until they are stiff and glossy (don't beat until "dry" looking). Use an electric mixer at high speed, or use a rotary beater, turning it as fast as possible. After the egg whites stand in soft smooth peaks, add the sugar very slowly, one tablespoon at a time, continuing to beat at medium speed. The baking instructions will be given with each recipe.

CRISP MERINGUES

1 cup sugar	1 teaspoon vanilla
3 egg whites	1 teaspoon vinegar
½ teaspoon baking powder	1 teaspoon water
⅛ teaspoon salt	

Put the egg whites, baking powder, salt, vanilla, vinegar and water into a large mixing bowl. Beat with electric mixer at high speed until the egg whites are stiff and glossy and stand in well formed peaks when beater blades are pulled up. Now add the sugar very slowly, 1 tablespoon at a time, continuing to beat at medium speed. Heap the meringue onto a greased baking dish from which it can be served or a baking pan with a removable rim. With a spatula shape the meringue into a shell, smooth off the bottom and build up a heavy rim. Bake it at 275° for 1¼ hours. To make small shells drop the meringue by the spoonful on a greased baking sheet and shape with a spatula or knife. To make "kisses", drop the meringue by the spoonful on a greased baking sheet and pull the meringue up into a peak or spiral with the spoon. For smaller meringues shorten the baking time.

The meringue is not a dessert in itself, but the basis for a dessert. The shells are delicious filled with sweetened fresh or stewed fruit and topped with whipped cream. Fresh or frozen raspberries or strawberries are particularly good. Or try a combination of fruits such as peaches and blueberries, or strawberries and fresh pineapple. An easy and good way to present meringues is filled with ice cream smothered in chocolate sauce.

Two very successful fillings for meringues are lemon custard and cold chocolate filling. If you are going to use the latter, fold ½ cup of chopped nuts into the meringue before baking it.

LEMON CUSTARD FILLING

3 beaten egg yolks	½ cup water
½ cup sugar	1 cup heavy cream
Juice and rind of large lemon	¼ teaspoon vanilla
1½ tablespoons flour	Sugar

Combine all the ingredients in the top of a double boiler or in a heavy bottomed pan. Stirring constantly, cook over boiling water or over low heat until thick. Cool. Whip heavy cream until stiff, flavor with vanilla and sweeten to taste.

Spread the meringue with a thin layer of whipped cream, then spread on the lemon filling and cover it with the remaining whipped cream. Chill the tart for at least 5 hours before serving.

COLD CHOCOLATE FILLING

2 squares bitter chocolate (2 oz.)
3 tablespoons sugar
¼ cup condensed milk
¼ teaspoon salt

3 egg yolks, beaten
1 pint heavy cream, whipped
1 teaspoon vanilla

Melt the chocolate over hot water. Stir in the sugar, condensed milk and salt. Place the pan over low heat and stir until the sugar is dissolved. Gradually add the beaten egg yolks, cook and stir until thickened. Cool the mixture, and then fold in the whipped cream and vanilla. Pile lightly in the meringue shell which has had ½ cup chopped nuts added to it before baking.

SOFT MERINGUE TOPPING

There are few desserts so mouthwatering as a pie with a really high, beautiful meringue topping. And you do not have to be a professional cook to produce one. For a 9 inch pie:

4 egg whites
¼ teaspoon salt
½ teaspoon cream of tartar

8 tablespoons sugar
1 teaspoon vanilla

Place the egg whites and salt in a large mixing bowl and beat until just frothy. Add the cream of tartar and beat at high speed with an electric mixer or as fast as you can with a rotary beater, until the egg whites are stiff and form a nice peak when pulled up. Beat in the sugar, 1 tablespoon at a time. Add the vanilla and continue to beat for 1 minute. Pile the meringue lightly on the filled pie, higher in the center than toward the edges. It should be at least 2 inches deep at the center and $\frac{1}{2}$ to 1 inch deep at the edges. Be certain that the meringue goes right up to the crust so that there are no air spaces. Bake at 300° for 15 to 20 minutes. Permit the pie to cool slowly. If cooled rapidly, it will "weep". Do not put it into a refrigerator until at least 2 hours after removing it from the oven.

There are innumerable pie fillings to put under this meringue. I will give the recipes I have found most satisfactory for the three most popular: coconut cream, banana cream and lemon.

COCONUT CREAM PIE

1 baked 9 inch pie shell (page 98).	1 tablespoon butter
4 egg yolks	2⅓ cups scalded milk
½ cup sugar	1 teaspoon vanilla
¼ teaspoon salt	1 cup grated or shredded coconut
3 tablespoons cornstarch	Soft meringue topping (page 132).

Prepare one pie shell. Beat the egg yolks well, then beat in gradually the sugar, salt and cornstarch. Stir a little of the hot milk into the egg mixture and then gradually stir the warmed egg mixture into the milk. Cook and stir this custard over low heat until it is smooth and thick. Remove from the heat and stir in the butter, vanilla and coconut. Allow the filling to cool before putting it into the baked 9 inch pie shell. Cover the filling with meringue. Bake at 300° for 15 to 20 minutes or until delicately brown and set. Cool at room temperature. Chill before serving.

BANANA CREAM PIE

Prepare a baked 9 inch pie shell (page 98). Make the custard as for coconut cream (as above). Peel and cut 2 large ripe bananas into thin slices and fold them into the cooled custard. Fill baked pie shell, cover with meringue (page 132) and bake at 300° for 15 to 20 minutes. Cool at room temperature. Chill before serving.

LEMON MERINGUE PIE

1 baked 9 inch pie shell (page 98)	2 tablespoons butter
1⅓ cups sugar	⅔ cup lemon juice
5 tablespoons cornstarch	2 teaspoons grated lemon rind
⅛ teaspoon salt	(optional)
1½ cups water	Soft meringue topping (page 132)
6 beaten egg yolks	

Prepare one pie shell. Combine the sugar, cornstarch, salt and water in a heavy sauce pan. Cook and stir these ingredients over low heat until the mixture thickens. Continue to cook, stirring constantly, for 4 minutes. Stir a little of the hot mixture slowly into the well beaten egg yolks. Then stir the warmed egg yolks slowly into the mixture in the pan and continue to cook and stir for 3 minutes. Remove it from the heat and beat in the butter, lemon juice and rind. Cool the custard. Pour it into a baked 9 inch pie shell and cover with meringue. Bake at 300° for 15 to 20 minutes or until golden and set. Cool at room temperature for at least 2 hours. Chill before serving.

BAKED ALASKA

Baked Alaska requires a soft meringue, made just as the meringue for pie topping except that it must be baked in a very hot oven. This you can do safely, for it is whisked straight from the oven to the serving platter—served and eaten before you've had time to worry about its shrinking or weeping.

Baked Alaska, although a most impressive dessert, is very

easy to make. The only drawback is that it has to be assembled and baked at the last moment, so in a maidless household the hostess must absent herself from the table to prepare it.

Prepare soft meringue according to directions on page (132). For six individual servings double the recipe. Now cover a wooden board, such as a bread board, with heavy paper— a brown store bag opened up and cut to size does beautifully. Place on it slices of sponge cake or angel food cake 4 by 5 inches in size and $\frac{1}{2}$ inch thick. Place on each piece of cake a slice of ice cream cut 1 inch thick and 1 inch shorter and narrower than the cake so that the cake will protrude $\frac{1}{2}$ inch all around. Cover the ice cream and cake well with meringue. Be certain there are no holes or air spaces. The ice cream must be well insulated or it will melt. Bake the Alaska at 475° until the meringue is well browned, about 7 to 15 minutes. Serve immediately.

One large slice of cake may be used with a whole brick of ice cream. To add variety and flavor to the Alaska, you may hollow out the ice cream slightly and fill it with fresh or frozen fruit before covering it with the meringue.

CHOCOLATE ANGEL FOOD CAKE

Although lovely to look at, angel food cake by itself can be quite dull. It needs dressing up for flavor, either fruit with whipped cream or ice cream and a sauce. However, if you add a bit of cocoa to the batter, you have an angel food that needs only whipped cream and garnish of sweet chocolate to be party fare. Even though you may not agree with me on the blandness of plain angel food, you will find this chocolate flavored one a nice change.

1¼ cups egg whites (10 to 12 egg whites) (12 oz.)	½ teaspoon salt
	1 teaspoon cream of tartar

1½ cups sugar

½ teaspoon vanilla

¾ cup sifted cake flour (2 oz.)

¼ cup sifted cocoa (2 tablespoons)

3 cups sweetened whipped cream

Shaved sweet chocolate

The egg whites should be at room temperature. Put the egg whites and salt into a large mixing bowl and beat until just frothy. Add the cream of tartar and beat at high speed on an electric mixer or as fast as you can with a rotary beater until they are stiff but not dry. Gradually beat in 1 cup of the sugar, 1 teaspoonful at a time. Add the vanilla and beat for 1 minute more. Sift flour, cocoa and remaining sugar together 4 times. Now gently and gradually, ¼ cup at a time, fold the flour mixture into the egg whites. Pour the batter into an ungreased 9 inch tube pan. Bake it at 375° for about 35 minutes. Remove the pan from the oven and invert it over a cake rack. Allow it to cool for at least two hours before removing it from the pan. When ready to serve, split the cake into three layers, put it together again with sweetened whipped cream, cover the top and sides with whipped cream and garnish with shaved or grated sweet chocolate.

OLD-FASHIONED CHOCOLATE CAKE

In this day of one bowl cake making or prepared mixes, this recipe may seem a bit laborious. However, if you are nostalgic for chocolate cake the way mother made it, it will be worth the extra effort.

1½ cups sugar (12 oz.)

½ cup butter (4 oz.)

1 egg, beaten

2 cups sifted cake flour (7½ oz.)

1½ teaspoons cream of tartar

½ teaspoon salt

½ cup milk (4 oz.)

¾ cup boiling water (6 oz.)

1 teaspoon soda

2 squares melted chocolate

Cream the sugar and butter together, add the beaten egg and beat the mixture vigorously by hand or for 2 minutes at medium speed on the electric mixer. Sift together the sifted flour, salt and cream of tartar. Add the dry ingredients to the butter mixture alternately with the milk, beating vigorously after each addition by hand or on medium speed of mixer. Combine the soda with the boiling water, pour into the batter and blend in. Add the melted chocolate and continue beating until well blended. The batter will be thinner than most cake batters. Pour batter into a well greased loaf cake tin. Bake at 350° for 40 minutes. Frost with a rich chocolate icing. Do not try to remove the whole cake from the pan as it will crumble, cut and remove by the piece.

Yeast Doughs

WORKING with yeast dough does require a certain touch. But that touch is not difficult to acquire. Once you get the "feel" of handling yeast dough, you've opened the way to more baking pleasure than you may have expected. Practice is the key to success, but if you follow the directions carefully you will never have a failure and, much more important, your products will improve each time you make them. Before long you get the "feel", and from then on each effort will yield a perfect result. Practically all breads and rolls can be frozen, so when you have the urge and the time, bake enough to stock the freezer and eat them when you are hungry for them.

CROISSANTS

A delicate flaky butter-rich roll that is common breakfast fare on the Continent, particularly in France. Croissants with strawberry jam, a cup of good coffee—I can think of no more delightful way to start the day. Except in the specialty pastry shops in the larger cities, croissants are commercially unobtainable in the States. This is understandable; for they are not good unless made with lots of sweet butter and are given many turns before baking.

I must warn you not to attempt to bake croissants on a hot

summer day, for the butter will melt before it has a chance to
be worked into the dough.

2 cups sifted all purpose flour	¾ cup cold milk (6 oz.)
1 yeast cake or envelope dry yeast (⅗ oz.)	1 egg yolk
	1¼ sticks sweet butter (5 oz.)
2 tablespoons warm water	1 beaten egg yolk
2 tablespoons sugar	1 tablespoon cold milk
¼ teaspoon salt	

Sift the flour into a large mixing bowl. In a small bowl soften
the yeast in lukewarm water. Work about 3 tablespoons of the
sifted flour into the yeast to make a soft dough. Form it into a
ball and cut a cross in the top. Cover the bowl with a towel
and put in a warm place for ½ hour or until almost double in
bulk.

Add the sugar and salt to the remaining flour. Put an egg
yolk into a cup, stir a bit with a fork, add cold milk to the cup
until it is ¾ full. Gradually add the milk and egg yolk mixture to the flour, working it in with your hands to make a
firm dough. Flour a board lightly and flatten out this dough on
it. Put the raised yeast dough on it. Fold over to cover the
yeast dough and knead the two doughs together, folding the
edges toward the center and pushing down with the heels of
your hands until just blended together.

Again sprinkle the board lightly with flour and roll out the
dough into a long rectangle about ½ inch thick. Wash the
sweet butter well under cold running water or in a bowl of ice
water until it is a smooth paste: to do this, pinch the butter
through your fingers either under the running water or under
the ice water in a bowl until it is very pliable, then slap it
back and forth in your hands until you have shaken off the
excess water. Be sure all the butter is pliable for if there are any
hard little lumps, these will not work nicely into layers in the
dough. Also, be certain the butter remains cold, or it will run
out rather than work into the dough.

Now form the butter into a flat cake and place it in the center of the dough. Fold one third of the dough over the butter, then the other third on top to make three layers. Turn the dough so that one of the open ends faces front. Roll it out again into a long rectangle, fold in thirds as before and again turn so that open end faces front. This folding, rolling out and turning operation is called a turn.

You may find the dough hard to work with at this point. Butter does on occasion break through or the whole mass may become slippery and sticky, but after it has been refrigerated it will become more manageable and each turn will make it smoother. Be sure to keep your working surface lightly floured, sprinkling on a little additional flour after each turn.

Wring out a towel or napkin in cold water, wrap the dough in it and place it in the refrigerator for at least 2 hours. The dough may be refrigerated overnight.

After several hours, or the next day, roll out the dough, fold and turn. Chill and give dough two more turns. Chill the dough for at least 1 hour before shaping it for baking.

Cut the dough in half and roll out each part, one at a time, into a circle $\frac{1}{8}$ inch thick and about 10 to 12 inches in diameter. Cut the circle as a pie into 7 or 8 triangles. Starting with the broad end of the triangle, roll each section, not too tightly, to form a cigar-shaped roll, thicker in the middle than at the ends. Curve the ends a bit to form crescents. Place them on a baking sheet rinsed in cold water, cover with a towel and let rise in a warm place for 20 minutes. If you want a glaze, brush the tops with a mixture of 1 egg yolk, beaten with a tablespoon of cold milk. Bake for 12 to 15 minutes at 400°.

Serve warm. Croissants can be baked in advance and reheated before serving. If you wish to make them in quantity, you can freeze them and defrost and heat as you want.

DANISH PASTRY

Danish pastry is well known and available in most bakeries in one form or another—sometimes very good, sometimes not so good and sometimes misnamed. In any case, I think you will find it worth the effort to make your own, for these pastries are better than it is usually possible to obtain commercially.

3 tablespoons all purpose flour
(1⅓ oz.)
5 ounces (1¼ sticks) sweet butter
⅛ cup lukewarm water (1 oz.)
1 yeast cake or envelope dry
yeast (⅗ oz.)
1 tablespoon sugar
1 beaten egg
1½ tablespoons sugar

½ cup cold milk
1¾ cups all purpose flour, sifted
(7 oz.)
Cinnamon and sugar, mixed
Nuts and raisins (optional)
Confectioners' sugar
Cream or milk
Vanilla

Wash the sweet butter under running cold water or in a bowl of ice water until it is very pliable. Do this by squeezing the butter through your fingers under the water. Slap the butter back and forth between your hands to shake off excess water.

Sift 3 tablespoons flour onto the butter and with your fingers work the flour thoroughly into the butter. Wrap up the dough in wax paper and chill in the refrigerator while mixing the other ingredients.

Soften the yeast in lukewarm water with 1 tablespoon sugar for 10 minutes. Stir in the beaten egg, 1½ tablespoons sugar and cold milk. Gradually add the sifted flour, beating well as you add it until the dough is smooth and shiny. The dough should not be sticky, so pick it up and roll it on a floured board, folding it over until it no longer sticks to your fingers. Roll out the dough on a floured board into an 8 inch square. Flatten out the chilled butter dough and place this over one half the dough. Fold the other half of the dough over this and pinch the edges together. Now roll it out into a long rectangle about $\frac{1}{2}$ inch thick. Fold one third of the dough over the center and then fold the remaining third on top of this, making three layers. Turn the dough so that the open end faces front. Roll out again into a long rectangle and repeat the folding operation and turn. Wrap the dough in waxed paper and chill for at least 2 hours or as long as overnight. Give the dough three more turns, roll into a long rectangle, fold in thirds and turn three times. Chill the dough for at least an hour before shaping.

Roll out the dough into a square $\frac{1}{4}$ inch thick and sprinkle with cinnamon and sugar, and nuts or raisins if you wish. Cut the dough in half and place one half on top of the other and roll up the two layers like a jelly roll. Cut the roll into slices $\frac{1}{2}$ inch thick and place on a buttered baking sheet. Cover lightly with a towel and chill for 2 hours or more before baking. This pastry is not allowed to rise in a warm place. Remove from the refrigerator and bake immediately in a 400° oven for 8 minutes. Reduce heat to 350° and bake for 10 more minutes or until slightly golden. Be careful not to overbake.

Frost while hot with confectioners' sugar and a little cream or milk mixed to a thick paste and flavored with vanilla. If you wish, sprinkle top with nuts or put a teaspoon of jam in the center of each roll.

These, too, can be baked ahead of time and reheated before serving, or can be baked and kept in the freezer until you want them.

BRIOCHE

A tender, slightly firm, egg-rich roll which, along with the croissant, is the mainstay of the French breakfast.

Recipes for the brioche, as it is made in France, not only sound complicated but are complicated. Unless warned, you would think you had done something drastically wrong, for from beginning to end the dough looks and feels somewhat messy and cannot be handled as most yeast doughs can.

2 cups all purpose flour (8 oz.)	1 tablespoon milk
1 envelope dry yeast or yeast cake ($\frac{3}{5}$ oz.)	$\frac{1}{4}$ cup ($\frac{1}{4}$ pound) butter
$\frac{1}{4}$ cup lukewarm water (2 oz.)	3 eggs
$\frac{1}{2}$ teaspoon salt	1 egg yolk
1 tablespoon sugar	1 tablespoon water

Sift the flour onto a board or into a large mixing bowl. Dissolve the yeast in the lukewarm water and then mix into it $\frac{1}{3}$ to $\frac{1}{2}$ cup of the sifted flour, enough to form a soft paste or dough. Roll this paste into a ball, cut a cross on top, place it in a small bowl, cover and set in a warm place for 30 minutes or until double in bulk.

Then make a hollow in the remaining flour, put into it the salt, sugar, milk and one-third of the butter. (Have the butter rather soft.) Add 2 of the eggs. Begin by thoroughly mixing the butter, eggs and seasoning. Then pull in the flour slowly and combine with the ingredients in the hollow. When the paste forms a compact mass, flour your hands and knead the dough and pull it about as much as you can to give it a certain elasticity. If you feel it looks more like a child's mish-mash than a respectable dough, don't despair, it is all in the nature of brioche. Now again make a hole in the center of it and add the last egg. Mix it into the paste and work it again with your hands. When the egg is worked in, add the remaining butter, softened to about the same consistency as the paste. Knead the butter and paste together until completely combined. At this point turn the paste onto a lightly floured board and spread the yeast dough on top of it. Mix the two doughs together. Gather up the dough into a ball (you will need a spatula to scrape some of it off the board and well floured hands to handle it) and place it in a lightly floured bowl. Cover and let rise in a warm place for 4 hours. It will then be more than double in bulk. With the aid of a rubber scraper turn the dough out onto a floured board and beat it with the flat of the scraper or the palm of your hand. Again gather it up into a ball, return it to the bowl, cover and allow to rise in a warm place for another 4 hours. Turn out onto a floured board again and knead down, then beat for 3 minutes with the flat side of a rubber scraper or palms of your hands. To make individual brioche (*les petites brioches*) pinch off enough dough to half fill a greased muffin tin or a fluted brioche mold. Then take a smaller amount of dough, about $\frac{1}{4}$ the amount, and roll into a pear shape. Indent the middle of the dough in the muffin tin and on it put the pear shape with the pointed side in the indentation. Cover the rolls with a towel, put in a warm place and let rise for 30 minutes or until double in bulk. Brush the tops of the rolls with a mixture of 1 egg yolk beaten with 1 tablespoon water. Bake at 400° for 10 minutes, then reduce heat to 350° and bake for another 10 minutes.

The dough may be baked in a large smooth mold. It is then called a Brioche Mousseline. Grease the mold and fill it two thirds full of the dough. Let rise and bake as the individual brioche.

BASIC SWEET DOUGH

A delicious light airy roll, equally good for dinner rolls or for sweet rolls and coffee cake. This is the comfortable sort of recipe you always come back to after experimenting with others.

1 package dry yeast ($\frac{2}{8}$ oz.)	$\frac{1}{2}$ cup lukewarm milk (4 oz.)
$\frac{1}{2}$ cup lukewarm water (4 oz.)	$1\frac{1}{2}$ tablespoons lemon juice
$\frac{1}{4}$ cup butter (2 oz.)	1 well beaten egg
$\frac{1}{3}$ cup sugar (2 $\frac{1}{2}$oz.)	$3\frac{1}{2}$ cups sifted all purpose flour
$\frac{1}{2}$ teaspoon salt	(14 oz.)

Pour the lukewarm water over the yeast, stir and let stand for 10 minutes. Cream together the butter, sugar and salt; stir in the beaten egg and lemon juice. Add the lukewarm milk to the yeast mixture, blend in $1\frac{1}{2}$ cups of the sifted flour and beat until very smooth. Combine the flour mixture with the butter mixture and mix well. Gradually add the remaining flour until you have a medium soft dough. You may not need all the flour. Toward the end of mixing in the flour use your hands and as soon as the dough can be handled without sticking, you have enough flour. The dough must be as light as it is possible to keep it without being sticky. Place the dough on a lightly floured board and knead it for 3 minutes by pushing the edges into the center with the heels of the hands. Gather the dough into a ball and place it in a greased bowl. Cover with a towel and let rise in a warmish place until double in bulk, about 2 hours. Punch down the dough by putting your fist into the middle of it, pick it up and roll again into a ball its original size. You can now roll out and shape the dough as you desire and let rise for baking, or you can put it in a covered bowl and store in the refrigerator for later use. The dough can be stored for as long as 3 days. It will rise a little while in the refrigerator. After shaping, let rise from $1\frac{1}{2}$ to 2 hours or until double in bulk. Bake at 400° for 5 minutes, reduce heat to 350° and bake another 10 to 15 minutes until delicately brown.

PARKER HOUSE AND CLOVER-LEAF ROLLS

For Parker House rolls, roll out the above dough $\frac{1}{3}$ inch thick, cut into rounds with a $2\frac{1}{2}$ or 3 inch cookie cutter or the floured rim of a glass. With the dull side of a knife make a deep impression across each round just a bit off center. Brush the smaller half of the round with melted butter and fold over so that the smaller half overlaps the larger. Put the rolls right next to each other on a greased baking sheet or, to make a very attractive ring, place them right next to each other forming a circle in a greased 9 inch round cake pan. Bake as directed for sweet dough. Gather up the scraps of dough and use them for making bow knots, or roll them into small balls and put three balls into each greased muffin tin to make clover-leaf rolls. Instead of cutting the dough into circles, you can cut it into triangles with 3 inch bases and about 4 inches long. Roll them loosely to form a cylindrical roll with tapered ends.

SWEET ROLLS

To make pecan rolls or other sweet rolls, roll out the sweet dough $\frac{1}{3}$ inch thick, spread with melted butter, sugar and cinnamon. You can add chopped pecans or raisins if you wish. Roll up the dough and cut into slices 1 to $1\frac{1}{2}$ inches thick and place side by side in a pan the bottom of which you have covered with butter, brown sugar and pecans. A variation in this is to cover the bottom of the pan with butter, honey and a drop of orange juice. After baking as directed for sweet dough turn out of the pan, upside down on to a plate, the minute you remove them from the oven. You can also place the cut slices of dough into muffin tins in which you have placed the butter and sugar mixture and bake as directed.

EASY ICE-BOX ROLLS

A simple, never fail, no knead roll. By simple I do not mean to deprecate its character, for it is an excellent light dinner roll. It is the perfect solution when you want the touch that only a good homemade roll can give a meal but don't have the time or energy to work with dough.

1 yeast cake ($\frac{3}{5}$ oz.)	1$\frac{1}{2}$ teaspoons salt
$\frac{1}{4}$ cup lukewarm milk (2 oz.)	1 tablespoon vegetable shortening
$\frac{1}{2}$ teaspoon salt	1 beaten egg
1 cup boiling water (4 oz.)	3$\frac{1}{4}$ to 4 cups sifted all purpose
$\frac{1}{4}$ cup sugar (2 oz.)	flour (approximately 1 lb.)

Dissolve the yeast cake in $\frac{1}{4}$ cup lukewarm water with $\frac{1}{2}$ teaspoon salt. In a bowl combine the boiling water, sugar, $1\frac{1}{2}$ teaspoons salt and vegetable shortening. Stir until shortening dissolves, cool to lukewarm, then stir in the beaten egg and the dissolved yeast. Add flour $\frac{1}{2}$ cup at a time and beat well after addition. When the dough is smooth and shiny, cover the bowl and put in the refrigerator for at least 6 hours or overnight. Three hours before baking, remove dough from the refrigerator and pinch off enough dough to fill greased muffin tins half full. If you wish to make clover-leaf rolls, place three small balls of dough in each muffin tin. Cover pans with a towel and place in a warm place for 3 hours. Bake for 15 minutes at 400°.

RICH COFFEE CAKE

This dough is too rich for dinner rolls, but if you don't require that your dough play two roles and are interested only in a delicious rich coffee cake, try this recipe.

$\frac{1}{2}$ cup all purpose flour (2 oz.)	$\frac{1}{2}$ teaspoon salt
1 tablespoon dry yeast or 1 yeast cake ($\frac{3}{8}$ oz.)	1 teaspoon grated lemon rind
	$1\frac{1}{2}$ tablespoons lemon juice
$1\frac{1}{2}$ teaspoons sugar	2 beaten eggs
$\frac{1}{2}$ cup lukewarm water (4 oz.)	$\frac{1}{2}$ cup milk
$\frac{1}{2}$ cup butter (4 oz.)	4 cups sifted all purpose flour (1 lb.)
$\frac{1}{2}$ cup sugar	

Place the $\frac{1}{2}$ cup flour into a large mixing bowl. Crumble the yeast cake over it or pour over it the dry yeast dissolved in the lukewarm water. Add the lukewarm water (if you used yeast cake) and $1\frac{1}{2}$ teaspoons sugar. Stir these ingredients until they are well blended. Cover them and set aside in a warm place for 30 minutes.

Beat together the butter and sugar; when smooth and creamy add the salt, lemon rind, lemon juice, beaten eggs and milk.

Combine the two mixtures and then stir in as much of the sifted flour as you can, working in the remainder of the flour with your hands. Knead the dough on a lightly floured board for 4 minutes. Place in a large greased bowl, cover with a towel and set in a warm place to rise for three hours.

Knead down the dough, roll, fill and shape as desired. Permit the shaped coffee cake to rise for 45 minutes in a warm place. Bake at 350° for 20 to 25 minutes or until golden and light to the touch. Allow to cool for a few minutes before frosting.

NO-KNEAD SWEET ROLLS

What can be more satisfying than a roll recipe guaranteed to produce a delicately light roll even if you are the rankest amateur in the baking department?

1 cup milk (8 oz.)
½ teaspoon salt
1 tablespoon shortening
1 egg

1 yeast cake (⅜ oz.)
¼ cup sugar (2 oz.)
3 cups all purpose flour (12 oz.)

Combine the milk, salt and shortening and heat to the boiling point. Cool to room temperature. While the mixture is heating, dissolve the yeast in the sugar; just mix the yeast and sugar together and let stand until the yeast is dissolved. If you use dry yeast dissolve it in ¼ cup lukewarm water and then add the sugar. When the milk mixture is cool, stir in the yeast and the unbeaten egg. Blend in the flour. After the first 2 cups of flour the dough will be too heavy for stirring, so work in the remainder with your fingers. You may need a little additional flour to reach the point where the dough no longer sticks to the fingers. Cover the bowl with a towel and set in a warm place for 1½ hours or until dough is double in bulk. Toss the dough onto a lightly floured board and roll it out and shape as desired. Bake at 375° for 20 minutes.

STICKY BUNS

Follow the recipe for *No-knead Sweet Rolls* (page 148). Roll the dough ½ inch thick, spread it with softened butter or margarine, sprinkle it generously with sugar and cinnamon, roll as a jelly roll and cut into 1 inch slices. Place these slices, cut side down, side by side in a square cake pan that has the bottom well covered with melted butter or margarine and brown sugar and 4 tablespoons water. Pecans may be spread over the butter and brown sugar mixture. Raisins may be spread on the dough before rolling it. Cover the pan of rolls with a towel, again set in a warm place and permit the rolls to rise for 1½ hours. Bake at 375° for 20 minutes.

KUCHEN

1½ cups milk (12 oz.)	1 cup sugar (8 oz.)
¾ cup melted vegetable shortening (6 oz.)	¼ cup lukewarm water
1¼ teaspoons salt	6 cups sifted all purpose flour (1½ lb.)
1 yeast cake (⅝ oz.) or package dry yeast	3 egg yolks, well beaten

Heat the milk to the boiling point. Combine milk, melted shortening, 2 tablespoons of the sugar and the salt. Cool to lukewarm. Dissolve the yeast in the lukewarm water. When milk mixture is cooled, add the yeast and beat in 3 cups of the flour. Cover the dough and set in a warm place to rise for 2 hours or until light and bubbly. Beat into the dough the remaining sugar, the beaten egg yolks and the remaining flour. Toss the dough onto a floured board and knead until smooth. Return to a large greased bowl, cover and allow to rise for 2 hours or until double in bulk. Punch the dough down, toss onto floured board and roll out ½ inch thick. Shape and fill

as desired, let rise for 1½ hours or until again double in bulk.
Bake at 375° for 20 minutes if made into rolls and 30 minutes
if shaped into a ring or coffee cake. These lend themselves well
to a simple butter, sugar and cinnamon filling with a teaspoon
of jam pressed into the top of each roll. Frost them after they
come out of the oven with a confectioners' sugar and cream
icing. Add just enough cream to the confectioners' sugar to give
it a spreading consistency.

This recipe makes a large batch of rolls or two good-sized
coffee cakes. Unless you have a large family or a freezer for
storing the excess, you may want to cut the recipe in half.

HOME-MADE BREAD

For those who object to the light gummy commercial bread
and remember with nostalgia the crusty fragrant bread mother
and grandmother used to make, the making of bread at home
will prove most rewarding. With bread, more than any other
yeast product, experience is more important than a given
recipe. I'm saying this to encourage you although it may
sound discouraging. If your first batch of bread doesn't fulfill
your expectations, don't give up; perhaps you didn't knead
it long enough or had the dough too stiff or not stiff enough.
Try another batch. Once you have gotten the feel of a good
dough you will easily make consistently good bread. I am
giving the two recipes I have found most satisfactory, one a
basic recipe for White Bread and one for a Sour Dough
White Bread. I think the latter is a bit more tasty. When you
become a confirmed bread maker, you will find it satisfying to
alternate the two.

WHITE BREAD

For two 4 by 8 inch loaves:

1 yeast cake (⅝ oz.) or 1 table-spoon or envelope dry yeast	1 cup scalded milk (8 oz.)
	1 cup hot water (8 oz.)

¼ cup lukewarm water
6 cups sifted all purpose flour
(1½ lbs.)

2 tablespoons shortening
2 tablespoons sugar
1 tablespoon salt

Dissolve the yeast in the lukewarm water. In a separate large bowl combine the milk, water, shortening, sugar and salt. When this mixture is lukewarm combine it with the dissolved yeast. Stir in slowly 3 cups of the flour, beat well and then add the remaining flour, working it in with your hands. Toss the dough on a floured board. Knead it well for about five minutes, folding the edges of the dough toward the center and pressing it down with the heels of your hands, adding a little more flour if it is sticky as you fold it over. Continue this folding and pressing until the dough no longer adheres to the board and is smooth and elastic. Shape the dough into a ball and place it in a large greased bowl. Cover with a towel and put in a warm place to rise until doubled in bulk, about 1½ hours. Knead it down to its original bulk and again let it rise until double, about 1½ hours. Pinch the dough in half and shape into two loaves, place them in greased bread tins filling the tins two thirds full. Let the loaves rise until they are double in bulk, rounded high and smooth above the tins. Bake at 450° for 10 minutes, reduce heat to 350° and bake for another 35 minutes. When done, the loaves will shrink from the sides of the pan and sound hollow when tapped. Remove the loaves at once from the pans and place on a wire rack or in some place where they will have air from all sides while cooling.

SOUR DOUGH WHITE BREAD

Starter

1 yeast cake or envelope dry
yeast (⅝ oz.)
½ cup lukewarm water
(4 oz.)

2 cups lukewarm water (16 oz.)
1 tablespoon sugar
1 tablespoon salt
2 cups sifted all purpose flour (½ lb.)

Bread

1 cup starter	1 tablespoon shortening
½ cup scalded milk (4 oz.)	3½ cups sifted all purpose flour
2 tablespoons sugar	(14 oz.)

To make the starter, sprinkle or crumble the yeast over ½ cup lukewarm water in a bowl, stir and let stand for 10 minutes. Add the 2 cups lukewarm water, sugar and salt. Stir in the sifted flour and beat together well. Cover the bowl with a plate and let it stand in a warm place for 3 days, stirring it down each day. After three days, measure 1 cup of the starter into a large bowl. Scald the milk and add the sugar and shortening. Cool to lukewarm and add to the starter. Gradually beat in the flour. Toss the dough onto a lightly floured board and knead it well for 3 minutes. Shape the dough into a ball, place it in a greased bowl, cover with a towel and let it rise in a warm place until doubled in bulk, about 1½ hours. Punch the dough down, reshape into a ball and let it rise again until double in bulk, about 45 minutes. Punch it down once more and then shape it into a loaf and place it in a greased bread tin. Cover with a towel and let the loaf rise in a warm place until double in bulk, about 1 hour. Bake at 400° for 50 minutes or until crisp and well browned.

Add to the remaining starter: 1 cup lukewarm water, ½ cup sifted flour and 1 tablespoon sugar. Set it aside until you are ready to make another batch of bread.

ENGLISH MUFFINS

English muffins are baked on a griddle, not in an oven. You will need not only a griddle, the same kind you use for pancakes, but also muffin rings made of strips of tin about an inch wide. The rings should be 3½ inches in diameter. If you cannot obtain these simple rings at your local hardware or household supply store, you can have them made at a tinner's or at any metal working shop. Or better, have your husband make them for you.

1 cup boiling water (8 oz.)	1 yeast cake or envelope dry yeast
1 cup scalded milk (8 oz.)	(⅜ oz.)
2 tablespoons sugar	¼ cup lukewarm water (2 oz.)
1 teaspoon salt	4 cups sifted all purpose flour (1 lb.)
3 tablespoons butter	

Combine the boiling water, hot milk, sugar, salt and butter in a large mixing bowl. Stir until the butter and sugar are dissolved. Allow to cool until lukewarm. In a separate bowl dissolve the yeast in the lukewarm water, allow it to stand for 10 minutes and then stir it into the milk mixture. Gradually stir in the sifted flour. When the flour is well blended with the liquid mixture, cover the bowl with a damp cloth. Place the bowl in a warm place to rise for 1½ to 2 hours or until the sponge dough falls back in the bowl, literally collapses. Grease ten 3 to 4 inch muffin rings and place them on a well-floured board. Fill them half full with the batter and allow to stand until the dough rises to the top. Grease a griddle generously with a saltless shortening and heat until quite hot. Lift the muffins from the board with a wide spatula or pancake turner onto the griddle. Turn the heat down and permit the muffins to bake slowly about 15 minutes to a side or until they are done. To serve, split them in half, butter and toast until golden brown. Accompany the muffins with jam or cream cheese or, better yet, with both.

SALLY LUNNS

The more attractive food looks the better it tastes. Sally Lunn is no exception. Even though it is good baked in any old cake or bread pan, it is better when baked in a fluted pan, one at least 4 inches deep.

1 yeast cake or envelope dry yeast (⅔ oz.)	2 tablespoons sugar
1 cup lukewarm milk (8 oz.)	2 beaten eggs
3 tablespoons butter	3½ cups all purpose flour (14 oz.)
	1 teaspoon salt

Dissolve the yeast in the warm milk. Cream together the butter and sugar. Add the beaten eggs and mix well. Combine the flour and salt. Now sift into the egg mixture the flour alternately with the milk and yeast mixture. Mix well together but do not knead. Put the dough into a greased bowl, cover with a towel and allow it to rise in a warm place until double in bulk. Turn the dough into a greased pan, allow to rise until it regains its bulk, about ½ hour, and bake at 300° for 1 hour or until it is golden brown. Serve warm with butter and jam. If you do not plan to eat it immediately, remove from the pan and allow to cool on a rack. Reheat it before serving.

Quick Breads

NON-YEAST COFFEE CAKE

This is the best non-yeast coffee cake I've eaten and the easiest to make.

2 cups sifted cake flour (½ lb.)
1½ cups sugar (12 oz.)
3 teaspoons baking powder
¼ pound butter or margarine
½ teaspoon salt
3 eggs, well beaten

¾ cup milk
1 teaspoon vanilla
⅔ cup chopped pecans or walnuts
2 tablespoons cinnamon mixed with
4 tablespoons sugar

Into a mixing bowl resift the sifted cake flour with the sugar, baking powder and salt. Cut in the butter and mix well with a pastry blender until the consistency of a very coarse meal. Gradually add the well beaten eggs mixed with the milk and vanilla. Blend together thoroughly.

Pour the batter into two greased and lightly floured 8 inch square cake pans. Sprinkle the top of the batter with a mixture of the chopped nuts, cinnamon and sugar. Bake at 375° for 30 minutes. This coffee cake, like most coffee cakes, is best served warm. It is as good reheated as direct from the oven and nice to have on hand in your freezer.

ORANGE LOAF

This orange loaf falls half-way between the bread and cake categories. It is one of those never fail recipes, simple to make and most satisfyingly good. It is ideal for a morning coffee snack, afternoon tea or a light luncheon dessert.

½ cup butter or margarine (4 oz.)	¼ teaspoon salt
1 cup sugar (8 oz.)	2 cups sifted all purpose flour
2 eggs, well beaten	1 teaspoon vanilla
½ cup raisins	
Grated rind of 2 oranges	*Topping*
⅔ cup sour milk	½ cup orange juice
1 teaspoon soda	¼ cup sugar
¼ teaspoon baking powder	

Cream together the butter and sugar. Add the beaten eggs and mix well. Add the raisins and grated orange rind. Add the soda to the sour milk. Add the baking powder and salt to the sifted flour. Add the sour milk and flour mixture alternately to the creamed mixture, stirring well after each addition. Lastly, stir in the vanilla. Pour the batter into 2 greased bread tins (4 by 8 inches). Bake at 350° for 35 minutes. Remove from the oven and immediately pour over the hot loaves the mixture of orange juice and sugar. This cake stays moist and delicious for several days. It is particularly good served slightly warm. Keeps well in a freezer.

YOGURT LOAF CAKE

A delicious moist cake, rather the consistency of pound cake, that is excellent to serve at tea or as dessert accompanying fruit compote. The recipe makes two 8 inch loaves.

1 cup yogurt (8 oz.)
2 cups confectionary sugar (8 oz.)
1 cup butter at room temperature (8 oz.)

3 cups sifted all purpose flour (12 oz.)
5 eggs, separated
1 teaspoon baking powder
2 teaspoons lemon juice

Cream together in a large bowl the butter and confectionary sugar. Add the yogurt and mix well with a wooden spoon. Blend in the beaten egg yolks and lemon juice. Whip the egg whites until stiff but not dry and carefully fold into them $1\frac{1}{2}$ cups of the sifted flour. Gently combine the two mixtures and then fold in the other $1\frac{1}{2}$ cups of sifted flour. Pour the batter into 2 well greased 8 inch bread tins. Bake at 375° for 1 hour or until thoroughly done. Test for doneness with a wooden toothpick, the toothpick must come out clean.

SCONES

These English teatime favorites are very closely related to our baking powder biscuits, but since they contain eggs and cream, they are a slightly richer branch of the family.

2 cups cake flour (8 oz.)
3 teaspoons baking powder
2 tablespoons sugar
$\frac{1}{2}$ teaspoon salt

4 tablespoons butter
$\frac{1}{2}$ cup cream
2 beaten eggs

Sift the flour, baking powder, sugar and salt into a mixing bowl. With a pastry blender cut in the butter until it is the size of peas. Combine the beaten eggs and cream. Make a well in the middle of the dry ingredients and pour in the egg mixture. Combine with a few deft strokes. Gently lift the dough onto a lightly floured board and pat it until it is $\frac{3}{4}$ inch thick. Cut into rounds with a biscuit cutter or into squares or diamonds with a knife. Brush the tops with a little beaten egg and sprinkle with sugar. Bake at 450° until golden, about 15 minutes. Serve hot with butter and jam or honey.

POPOVERS

Popover recipes can be found in almost all standard cook-books and the recipes are all practically the same. The recipe is a very simple one, but most women marvel when they see a "popped" popover—they seem convinced that some conjuring trick is involved. I am including my recipe here, not because it is so different but because I want to assure all aspiring popover makers that not only is no trick involved but no special technique is called for. Just follow the very simple instructions, and I guarantee that the popover will pop mightily.

1 cup sifted all purpose flour	1 cup milk
¼ teaspoon salt	1 tablespoon melted butter
2 large eggs, well beaten	

Sift the flour and salt into a bowl. Combine the milk, well beaten eggs and melted butter. Stir the liquid slowly into the dry ingredients. Beat with a rotary beater until they are very well blended. Grease six ovenproof glass custard cups and fill them a little over half full with the batter. Place the cups on a cookie sheet to keep them from tipping in the oven. Bake at exactly 450° for 20 minutes, then reduce the heat to 350° and bake another 15 or 20 minutes or until dry. Remove them at once from the cups and puncture them to allow the steam to escape. If you use the old cast iron popover pans, you must preheat them until they are very hot. Popovers are undeniably best when served immediately, but they do very well reheated.